# ADVANCED
# BRIDGE

# ADVANCED
# BRIDGE

## A PRACTICAL GUIDE TO IMPROVING YOUR GAME

David Bird

southwater

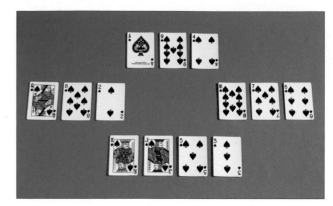

This edition is published by Southwater
an imprint of Anness Publishing Ltd
108 Great Russell Street
London WC1B 3NA
info@anness.com

www.southwaterbooks.com
www.annesspublishing.com

If you like the images in this book and would like to investigate using them for publishing, promotions
or advertising, please visit our website www.practicalpictures.com for more information.

Publisher: Joanna Lorenz
Project Editor: Sarah Doughty
Editors: Rosie Gordon and Felicity Forster
Photography: Paul Winch-Furness
Designers: Stuart Perry and Sylvia Tate
Production Controller: Pirong Wang

Previously published as part of a larger compendium,
*How to Play Winning Bridge: History, Rules, Skills & Tactics*

PUBLISHER'S NOTE
Although the advice and information in this book are believed to be accurate and true at the time
of going to press, neither the authors nor the publisher can accept any legal responsibility or liability
for any errors or omissions that may have been made nor for any inaccuracies nor for any loss, harm
or injury that comes about from following instructions or advice in this book.

PICTURE ACKNOWLEDGEMENTS
The publisher would like to thank the following for kindly supplying photos for this book:
David Bird: 61, 111, 123; Corbis: 124b, 125b, 112–13; Getty Images: 6t, 109b, 115t;
The Kobal Collection: 124t; PA Photos: 85b; Jonathan Steinberg: 119; TopFoto: 122b; World Bridge
Federation: 12t, 16, 23b, 29b, 41b, 49bl, 49br, 57b, 64t, 84b, 86t, 89r, 90b, 107b, 114t, 115r,
116r, 116l, 117t, 118l, 119b, 120b, 121t, 122t, 123b, 126t, 126b.
Every effort has been made to obtain permission to reproduce copyright material,
but there may be cases where we have been unable to trace a copyright holder.
The publisher will be happy to correct any omissions in future printings.

# CONTENTS

# INTRODUCTION

What is the world's greatest card game? Not everyone will give you the same answer but there are two clear frontrunners for the title – bridge and poker. Poker is as much about gambling as it is about tactical play. Bridge is quite different. It is sometimes played for money, yes, but it is also immensely stimulating intellectually. Although you can play and enjoy bridge after just a few hours of instruction, it is a game so deep that not even the greatest masters can claim to have learnt everything that the game has to offer.

A big attraction of the game is that it is played in partnership. You and your partner sit opposite each other at the card table, competing against two other players, also in partnership. However good you may be as a single player, you will not achieve very much without the cooperation of your partner. A long-term bridge partnership in many ways resembles a marriage. You must enjoy each other's company, maintain a pleasant relationship and refrain from criticism or argument, whatever bridge disasters you may experience.

Why do players in their millions take up this game and play it throughout their lives, scarcely able to imagine what "life without bridge" would be like? Firstly, it is a wonderful way to make friends. If you choose to play bridge in the environment of your

**Above:** Bridge tournament in progress. The player with her back to the camera is the declarer and the face-up cards, on the table opposite her, are those of the dummy.

home and your friends' homes, you will build a circle of close friends who meet perhaps once a week, play bridge and greatly enjoy each others' company. Perhaps instead you join the local bridge club. Immediately you will have a new group of acquaintances. There will never be a shortage of anything to talk about. Whenever bridge players meet, they can chat happily for hours, discussing exciting hands that they have played. It's the same if you visit an unknown country or town. You can present yourself at the local bridge club and receive an immediate welcome.

It may be that you are competitive. In that case bridge is just the right game to learn. You will begin by entering competitions at your local club and then advance to local championships. If you have some aptitude for the game and work hard, you may eventually play in national competitions. For the favoured few, there are European and world championships to be won.

## A deal of bridge

In bridge, the deal consists of two parts. First the four players, each looking only at their own hand of 13 cards, conduct an auction of ever ascending "bids". For example, a player might bid "one heart" to tell his partner that he holds an above average collection of high cards (aces, kings, queens and jacks) and that

**Above:** Most players sort the cards in their hand so that all the cards in one suit are together, with the highest-ranking card on the left and the lowest-ranking on the right.

hearts is his longest suit and might therefore make a good trump suit. When a suit eventually becomes "trumps", it is more powerful than the other three suits; a low trump will defeat even an ace in one of the other three suits. When the bidding comes to an end, one or other partnership will have set themselves a target for the second part of the proceedings: the play. For example, they may have said they will attempt to make ten tricks with spades as trumps. The play begins and that partnership must then try to make the target of ten tricks. The two defenders will do their best to prevent it.

## Using this book

The aim of this book is to help intermediate and high-level players improve their skills in the wonderful game of bridge. The book begins with three chapters covering intermediate-standard bridge, explaining bidding, card play and defence. Next, there are three chapters showing how to use these skills at a more advanced level.

Apart from instruction, the book also contains a guide to famous bridge players around the world, past and present, and the deals they have played. From film star Omar Sharif to the USA's Helen Sobel, many outstanding figures have graced the bridge table.

Once you have absorbed the instruction in this book, you will already have become a better than average player. You may not find it an easy task, it is true, but if the game were a simple one it would not provide such endless fascination. You can be sure that something interesting will happen every time that you play. As well as playing around a table, it is possible to play bridge on the internet nowadays, even with players from the other side of the world.

By working on and improving your bridge skills, you are moving further along the path of your enjoyable and life-long journey. Good luck!

### BRIDGE IN PRINT
♠ ♥ ♦ ♣

The four players in a bridge game are called North, East, South and West, according to the seat that they occupy. During a session each player is likely to become the declarer (the player who attempts to make the contract) several times. As you read this book, you may be puzzled why South is always shown as the declarer. This is a convention followed by all bridge books and newspaper columns. The South cards are "nearest" to the reader and so allow him or her to imagine being the declarer as the play is described.

### THE HAND DIAGRAMS
♠ ♥ ♦ ♣

On the right you see a typical hand diagram. The bidding, which takes place before the play, is shown in the green table at the bottom. South makes the first bid of 1♥ (one heart) and the final bid of 4♥ becomes the contract. South will play the contract, trying to make ten tricks with hearts as trumps (which is what the bid of 4♥ means). South becomes the declarer and will play the cards both from the North hand, the dummy, which will be laid face-up on the table, and from his own hand. East and West will become the defenders and try to prevent the declarer from scoring ten tricks. If you are unfamiliar with basic terms such as "bid", "1♥", "tricks", "pass", "contract", "play the contract", "trumps", "defenders", "declarer", "dummy", do not worry. Everything is clearly explained in the section called *Starting Out (The Basics)*.

**Right:** South is the dealer. "Love all" means that neither side has scored a game.

LOVE ALL
DEALER SOUTH

**Above:** North (the hand at the top) and South (the hand at the bottom) are partners. West and East (left and right respectively) form the opposing partnership.

**Right:** South opened (made the first bid) with 1♥ and the next three players all made a bid too. South's second bid of 4♥ was followed by three passes – indicated by "End".

| West | North | East | South |
|------|-------|------|-------|
|      |       |      | 1♥    |
| 1♠   | 2♥    | 2♠   | 4♥    |
| End  |       |      |       |

# Chapter 1

# Intermediate bidding

You should always be reluctant to allow the opponents to choose trumps at a low level, particularly if they have found a trump fit. The first topic in this section on intermediate bidding will be "balancing", where the player in the pass-out seat bids without the normal values, to prevent the opponents from winning the auction too cheaply. The universally popular transfer responses to 1NT will be described, where you respond in one suit to show length in the next higher suit. Next the important topic of bidding slams is covered, in particular "control-showing cue-bids", where you bid a suit in which you hold an ace or a king rather than one where you have some length. After a discussion of three types of conventional double – negative, responsive and competitive doubles – the section ends with a discussion on sacrificing, where you bid a contract that you expect to fail. Your aim is to lose fewer points than you would if the opponents were allowed to make their contract instead.

**Right:** The right-hand opponent opened 1♥. To express this minor two-suiter, overcall 2NT (the Unusual No-trump convention).

# BALANCING

When the strength between the two sides is evenly divided, or nearly so, you should be very reluctant to let the opponents choose trumps at a low level. This is particularly the case if they have found a trump fit. When you are in the pass-out seat, you should consider making a call of some sort, even when your own hand is quite weak. The fact that the opponents have stopped low implies that your partner is likely to hold reasonable values. Making such a call, in the pass-out seat, is known as "balancing" or "protecting".

## Balancing against a one-bid

Suppose the bidding starts in this fashion

| West | North | East | South |
|------|-------|------|-------|
| 1♥ | Pass | Pass | ? |

and you hold one of these hands in the South seat:

**1**

East did not have enough to respond, so your partner may well hold 10 points or so. Rather than allow West to choose trumps, you should overcall 2♦ on (1). You would not be strong enough to overcall 2♦ in the second seat. In the protective seat, however, you are entitled to bid with around a king less than normal. It's the same on (2). An overcall of 1NT would

**2**

normally show a stronger hand but, in the protective seat, you may bid 1NT on around 11–14 points. If your partner happens to hold 12 points himself, you may be able to make game.

**3**

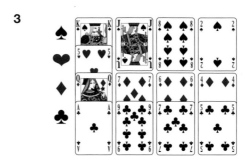

Hand (3) is worth a double. You would be reluctant to double in the second seat, with only 10 points. In the protective seat you can be bolder. Since you may be three points lighter than normal for any action taken in the protective seat, your partner should bid cautiously when advancing towards a possible game.

## Balancing against a two-level fit

When the opponents have found a trump fit but stopped at the two-level, the odds are very favourable for balancing. Your side must hold something approaching half the strength in the pack. Since you are both relatively short in the opponents' suit, there is a good chance that you will have a playable fit yourselves somewhere. Suppose the bidding starts

| West | North | East | South |
|------|-------|------|-------|
| 1♦ | Pass | 2♦ | Pass |
| Pass | ? | | |

and you hold one of these hands in the North seat:

**1**

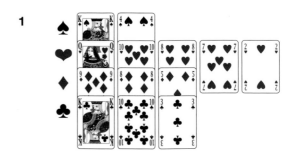

Compete with 2♥ on (1), rather than let the opponents choose trumps at the two-level. Do not worry that your partner, who is likely to hold around 10 points, will carry you too high. Remembering that you did not overcall 1♥ on the first round, he will realize that you are bidding the combined values of your own hand and his.

**2**

♠
♥
♦
♣

Similarly, you should bid 3♣ on (2). The opponents will often then bid 3♦, which may go down. On hand (3) you should double for take-out.

**3**

♠
♥
♦
♣

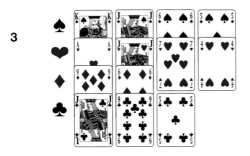

When you hold the minor suits and the opponents have found a fit in a major, you can use 2NT (the Unusual No-trump) to ask partner to choose one of the minor suits.

| West | North | East | South |
|------|-------|------|-------|
| 1♥ | Pass | 2♥ | Pass |
| Pass | ? | | |

Sitting North, you hold one of these hands:

**1**

♠
♥
♦
♣

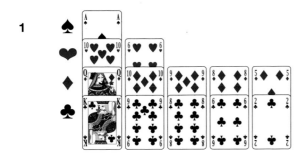

**2**

♠
♥
♦
♣

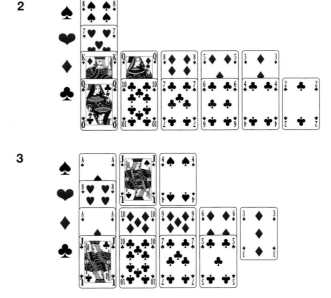

**3**

♠
♥
♦
♣

On hands (1) and (2) you would bid 2NT, asking partner to choose a minor. On hand (3) you would prefer to double, despite holding only three cards in the other major, spades.

**Above:** Dangerous to protect. Suppose you hold this hand and the opening 1♦ is followed by two passes. Ask yourself "Where are the spades?" Your partner did not overcall 1♠ and there is a risk that the opponents may find a spade fit if you bid. It is safer to pass.

---

### HESITATIONS
♠ ♥ ♦ ♣

Many disputes that arise during tournament play involve hesitations. It is perfectly acceptable to think for a while before making a bid or playing a card. You often give away information by doing so, however, particularly if you think for a while and then pass. Your partner must be particularly careful not to take advantage of the information gained.

# TRANSFER RESPONSES

**M**any social players, and nearly all tournament players, use "transfer responses" when partner has opened 1NT. A response of 2♦ shows at least five hearts and asks the opener to rebid 2♥. A response of 2♥ shows at least five spades and asks the opener to rebid 2♠. There are two big advantages of this method. The first is that the 1NT opener will play any contract in responder's five-card major. His hand will be hidden from view and his honour holdings will be protected from the opening lead. The second advantage is that after a start of 1NT – 2♦ – 2♥, the responder has a second chance to bid. He can continue with a further bid, such as 2NT, 3♦ or 3NT, having already shown five hearts.

Responder may use a transfer response to sign off in his long major. A transfer response does not promise any values at all. You may be very weak, intending to play in your long suit at the two-level. Or you may have a slam in mind. Here the responder has no ambitions:

**Above:** Oswald Jacoby, who originally conceived the idea of transfer responses in bridge.

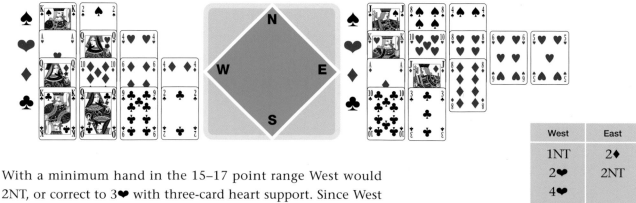

| West | East |
|------|------|
| 1NT | 2♦ |
| 2♥ | |

West opens a 15–17 point 1NT and East shows five hearts with a transfer response. Since he has no game ambitions, he passes the requested 2♥ rebid.

Because bidding 2♦ forces the opener to rebid 2♥, the responder has a chance to describe his hand further. If he continues with 2NT this will show the values to invite game:

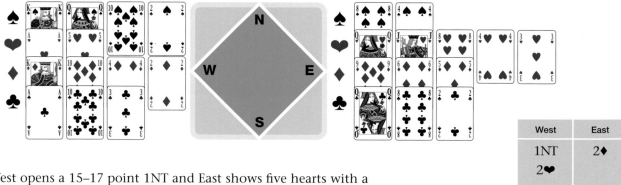

| West | East |
|------|------|
| 1NT | 2♦ |
| 2♥ | 2NT |
| 4♥ | |

With a minimum hand in the 15–17 point range West would pass 2NT, or correct to 3♥ with three-card heart support. Since West has 16 points, heart support and a possible ruffing value, he is happy to bid 4♥, accepting the game invitation.

The responder has these options after a start of 1NT – 2♦ – 2♥:

| Pass | no game ambitions |
|------|-------------------|
| 2♠ | natural and forcing |
| 2NT | inviting a game |
| 3♣/3♦ | natural and game-forcing |
| 3♥ | inviting a game, at least six hearts |
| 3NT | asking opener to choose between 3NT and 4♥ |
| 4♥ | to play. |

### Breaking the transfer

When the opener has four-card trump support and an upper-range hand, he should bid one level higher than normal. This is known as "breaking the transfer". Game may now be reached when responder was not quite strong enough to make a try himself:

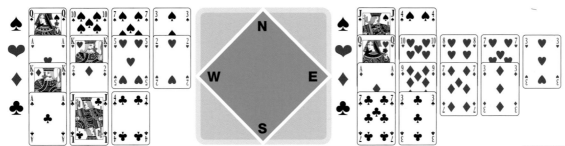

With just 7 points and a five-card suit, East would have passed a rebid of 2♥. When partner shows four-card heart support and an upper-range opening, East raises to game.

| West | East |
|------|------|
| 1NT | 2♦ |
| 3♥ | 4♥ |

### Transfers opposite a 1NT overcall

When partner has overcalled 1NT, it is a good idea for the responder to use Stayman and transfer bids.

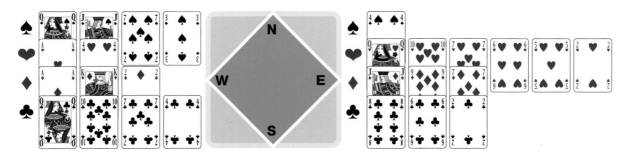

East has a weak hand and seeks sanctuary in his long heart suit.

### Transfers opposite a 2NT opening

A similar method is used opposite an opening bid of 2NT. A 3♦ response shows at least five hearts and asks opener to rebid 3♥. A response of 3♥ shows at least five spades and asks opener to rebid 3♠.

| West | North | East | South |
|------|-------|------|-------|
| | | | 1♦ |
| 1NT | Pass | 2♦ | Pass |
| 2♥ | End | | |

# Control-showing cue-bids

Suppose you have found a trump fit and have values to spare, so far as a game contract is concerned. You want to tell partner that a slam may be possible and to ask his view on the matter. It is not much use bidding some form of Blackwood. The meaning of a Blackwood bid is: "I know we have the values for a slam and I just need to check that there are not two aces missing." No, the only way to invite a slam, without going past the game-level, is to make a control-showing cue-bid. In other words, you bid a new suit (usually at the four-level or higher) after the trump suit has been agreed. This bid shows a control – an ace, king, singleton or void – in the suit that you have bid.

### Making a cue-bid with trumps agreed

Suppose the bidding has started like this:

| West | North | East | South |
|------|-------|------|-------|
| 1♠ | Pass | 3♠ | Pass |
| ? | | | |

You are sitting West. Partner has agreed spades as trumps and you have to assess slam prospects on the three hands shown below:

**1**

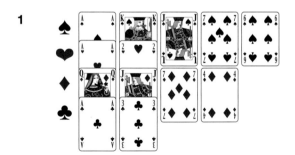

On (1) you can visualize a slam if partner has a diamond control. You make a control-showing cue-bid of 4♣. This passes the message: "I am strong enough to consider a slam and I have a control in the club suit." Your partner may now make a cue-bid himself, or perhaps sign off in 4♠. If he were to cue-bid 4♥, that would show a heart control. It would also deny a diamond control, since you show your cheapest control first. You would then sign off in 4♠, knowing that there were two top diamond losers.

**2**

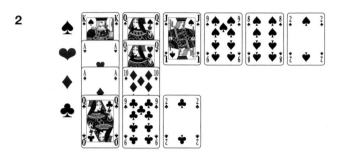

On (2) you would cue-bid 4♦, meaning: "I am strong enough to consider a slam and I have a control in diamonds but no control in clubs." If partner were to cue-bid 4♥, that would show a heart control and also a club control. Without a club control, he would have signed off in 4♠, knowing that there were two top losers in clubs.

**3**

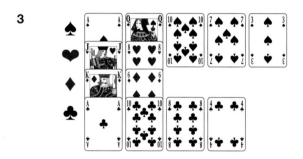

Hand (3) is not strong enough to suggest a slam, opposite partner's limit raise of 3♠, and you would bid 4♠.

Note that after a start of 1♠ – 2♠, a rebid of 3♣ by the opener would not be a cue-bid. Because the bidding has not yet been forced to game, a bid in a new suit is a game try. A bid in a new suit is a cue-bid only when the auction is already game-forcing.

---

### **Avoid the five-level**
♠ ♥ ♦ ♣

The secret of good slam bidding is to investigate a possible slam while the bidding is still below the game level. When the bidding starts 1♠ – 3♠ – 4♣ (where 4♣ is a control-showing cue-bid), a slam is suggested but the bidding can still stop in 4♠. Ideally, you should play in 4♠ or 6♠. To investigate a slam and then stop in 5♠ is to take an unnecessary risk of going down.

---

## Cue-bidding only with first-round control

The advantage of cue-bidding on both aces and kings, as just described, is that you can diagnose when you have two top losers in a suit. It is a method that was popularized by the great Italian teams of the 1970s. It does mean that you cannot be sure how many aces are held but, of course, you can usually bid Blackwood after making a cue-bid or two, thereby discovering whether there are two aces missing. Nevertheless, some partnerships prefer to make a cue-bid only when they hold a first-round control (the ace or a void). It is something that you must discuss with your partner.

## Agreeing a suit by making a cue-bid

On some auctions there is not enough space to explicitly agree partner's suit before making a cue-bid. When a bid at the four-level cannot logically be natural, it will be a cue-bid that agrees the suit last bid by partner. Let's see an example of this:

> **BLACKWOOD CONVENTION**
> ♠ ♥ ♦ ♣
>
> During a slam auction a bid of 4NT is the Blackwood convention, conceived by Easley Blackwood. It asks your partner how many aces he holds and the traditional responses are:
>
> 5♣ with none or four aces
> 5♦ with one ace
> 5♥ with two aces
> 5♠ with three aces

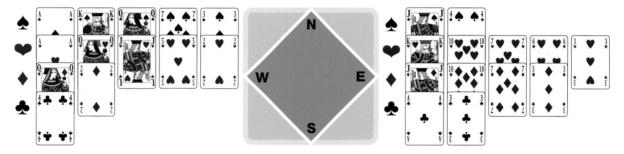

East has a super fit for hearts and indicates this by cue-bidding 4♣ instead of merely raising to 4♥. West has no diamond control, so he signs off in 4♥. Suppose West had held one diamond and two clubs instead. With the diamond suit controlled in his own hand, he would then have been much more interested in a slam. The bidding would have continued to the six-level:

| West | East |
|------|------|
| 1♠ | 1NT |
| 3♥ | 4♣ |
| 4♥ | |

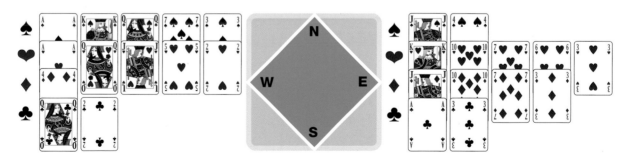

West uses the Blackwood 4NT convention, discovering that partner has one ace. He then bids a small slam in hearts, which is easily made.

You can see from this example how important it can be to show where you hold a control, rather than merely stating how many controls you have. Swap East's minors and he would have cue-bid 4♦ instead of 4♣. West would then know that there were two top losers in clubs and would sign off in game.

| West | East |
|------|------|
| 1♠ | 1NT |
| 3♥ | 4♣ |
| 4NT | 5♦ |
| 6♥ | |

# BIDDING SLAMS

The foundation of a successful slam auction has nothing to do with Blackwood or control-showing cue-bids. Both players must use the early rounds of the bidding to convey their general playing strength and to look for a trump fit. Only when both these tasks have been completed, and the playing strength for a slam has been confirmed, is it appropriate to check on controls.

## The requirements for a slam

Two elements are necessary to make a small slam. You must have the playing strength to make 12 tricks. You also need the controls to prevent the defenders from scoring two tricks.

Look at these two hands:

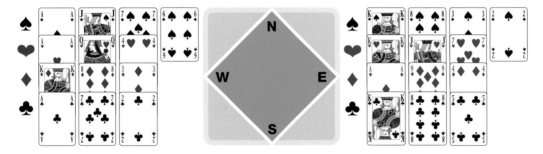

All the aces and all the kings are held, but there is insufficient playing strength for a slam. There are only 10 tricks on top and some luck will be required in the spade suit, even to score 11 tricks.

The next pair of hands contain playing strength in abundance but there is a flaw in the control situation:

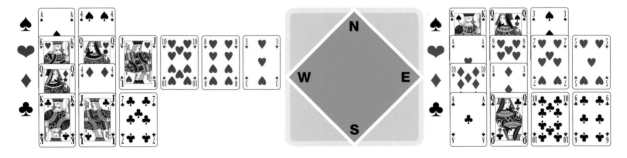

An excellent heart fit, with 13 top tricks. Unfortunately no diamond control is held and the defenders will be able to score the first two tricks.

## Assessing whether the power for 6NT is present

We will look first at how to assess whether the playing strength for a slam is present. To make 6NT when two balanced hands face each other, you will need 33 points or more. This is comparatively easy to judge. Once your partner has shown his own point-count, you simply add your own to assess the total. Let's see two typical slam auctions in no-trumps.

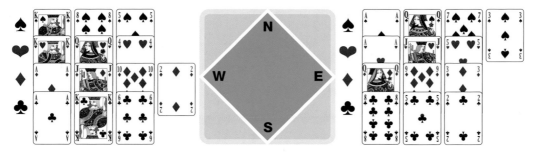

With 13 points opposite 20–22, East can be sure that the combined point total will be at least 33 points. He therefore leaps to 6NT. There are nine top tricks and the slam will be made if South holds the ♦K or the spades split 3–3.

| West | East |
|------|------|
| 2NT | 6NT |

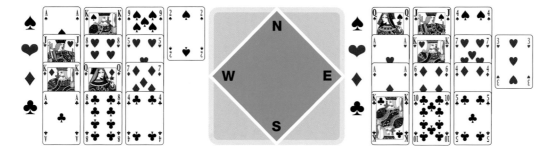

With 17 points facing a partner holding 15–17 points, East is not quite strong enough to jump to 6NT. He invites a slam by raising to 4NT. With a minimum hand for his strong no-trump, West would pass. Here he holds a maximum 17 points and therefore accepts the invitation, bidding 6NT. There are 11 tricks on top and you would seek a 12th by leading towards the ♥J, succeeding when South held the ♥Q or when hearts broke 3–3 (plus some other small chances).

| West | East |
|------|------|
| 1NT | 4NT |
| 6NT | |

### Assessing whether the power for a suit slam is present

It is somewhat more difficult to assess whether you have sufficient power to make a slam with a trump suit. High-card points are not so important as playing strength and the quality of the trump suit. In general, you should consider a slam when you have considerably more strength than you would need to raise to game.

There are several situations where the playing strength should be present for a slam, provided you can find a sound trump suit. Suppose the opener has a medium strength hand (16–18 points) and the responder has an opening bid himself. Provided a good trump fit can be found, the values for a slam should be there. The same is true when the responder has made a jump shift (for example 1♦ – 2♠) or when a positive response has been given to a 2♣ opening.

Remember that when partner opens 2♣ and rebids in a suit, he is showing that he has enough strength for a game in his own hand. If you hold an ace in your hand, or a king and a queen, this will often be enough to produce a slam.

**Above:** Lorenzo Lauria, senior member of the Italian team and winner of five world championships.

Here are some typical auctions investigating a slam contract:

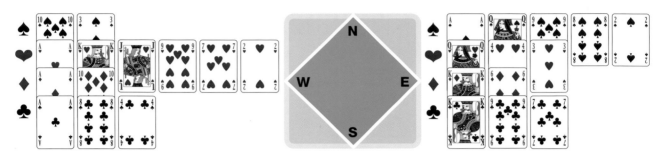

East has considerably more strength than would be needed to raise to 4♥ on the second round. Since he has a control in both the minor suits, he is happy to bid Blackwood. Partner shows three aces and the excellent small slam is reached. (In the later section on Advanced Bidding, we will look at Roman Key-card Blackwood, widely popular in tournament play, where the responses to 4NT identify not only the four aces but also the king and queen of trumps.) Even when a player has made a very strong bid, he may decide to sign off at the game-level when he is minimum for his call.

| West | East |
|------|------|
| 1♥ | 1♠ |
| 3♥ | 4NT |
| 5♠ | 6♥ |

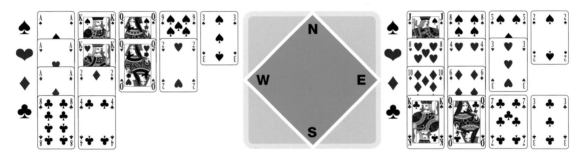

West bids just 4♠ to inform his partner that he has nothing to spare for a 2♣ opening. West has three losers in the minor suits and is confident that East will advance over 4♠ anyway, if he holds something like ♦K and the ♣A.

Let's make the West hand somewhat stronger by adding the ♦K:

| West | East |
|------|------|
| 2♣ | 2♦ |
| 2♠ | 3♠ |
| 4♠ | |

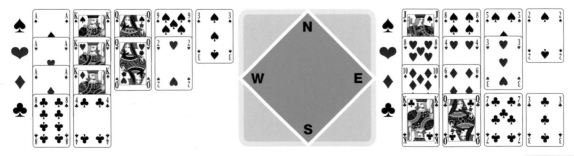

Now West suggests a slam by cue-bidding his diamond control. East is impressed by the fact that West has visualized a slam, despite holding no control in the club suit. He therefore shows his club control, bypassing the 4♠ safety level. This encourages West to jump to a small slam in spades.

| West | East |
|------|------|
| 2♣ | 2♦ |
| 2♠ | 3♠ |
| 4♦ | 5♣ |
| 6♠ | |

You can see that control-showing cue-bids have two purposes. Their main mission is to show a control in one of the side suits. They are used also to indicate a strong hand that is interested in a slam:

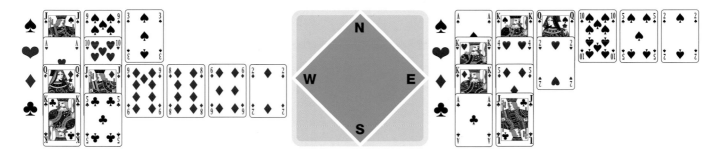

West has a minimum opening and no top honour in spades, the agreed trump suit. Nevertheless, he should be willing to cue-bid his ♥A because it does not carry the bidding past the next level of the trump suit (here 4♠). As it happens, this information is enough to persuade East to bid a slam. East knows that there cannot be a grand slam available, of course, because West's cue-bid in hearts denies the ♦A.

| West | East |
|------|------|
| 1♦ | 2♠ |
| 3♠ | 4♣ |
| 4♥ | 6♠ |

## Play in 6NT when the values are present

When you assess the combined point-count at 33 or more, it is usually wise to play in 6NT rather than in six of a suit. By doing so, you may avoid defeat when the suit that you would otherwise have chosen as trumps happens to break badly:

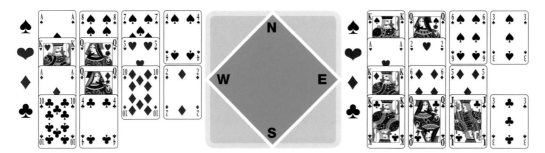

It is not a good idea to seek a spade fit by bidding Stayman on the East hand. The resultant contract of 6♠ will then go down when the spade suit breaks 4–1. Since East knows that 33–35 points are present, he should bid the slam in no-trumps. By doing so, he will also avoid the small chance of an adverse club ruff.

| West | East |
|------|------|
| 1NT | 6NT |

## Bidding a grand slam

The general advice about bidding grand slams is that you should do so only when you are confident that 13 tricks are present. Remember that if you fail in a grand slam you lose both the small slam bonus and the game bonus that you would otherwise have accrued. When playing duplicate it is particularly expensive to bid a grand slam and go one down, only to discover that your opponents stopped at the game-level on the same cards. You could then have obtained a big swing by bidding and making a small slam.

# NEGATIVE DOUBLES

In rubber bridge, where few conventions are played, the most common type of penalty double is that of an overcall, in an auction such as 1♠ – 2♦ – Dble. In tournament bridge, such doubles are almost universally played for take-out nowadays and are known as "negative doubles". The time has come to take a look at this method.

## The negative double

When you open with one of a suit and partner doubles an overcall up to the level of 3♠, this is for take-out. Such a double is known as a "negative double". (It was originally known as a Sputnik double, since it was conceived around the time of the Russian space satellite of that name.) It suggests that you have no accurate natural bid to make and that you hold one or both of the unbid suits.

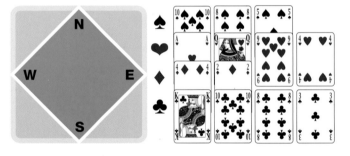

| West | North | East | South |
|------|-------|------|-------|
| 1♦ | 1♠ | Dble | |

East is strong enough to bid at this level but has no satisfactory natural bid to make. A response of 2♣ would overstate his values. He solves the problem by making a negative double. He strongly suggests four cards in the unbid major and may well have a club suit too. If partner rebids 2♣, 2♦ or 2♥, East will pass on this occasion. If instead he held 11 points or more he would show the additional strength by bidding again.

The higher the auction is, the more values a negative double will show. When the overcall is at the three-level, responder will need almost the values for making game:

**Above:** The double card. Nowadays a double card is used many more times for take-out than for penalties.

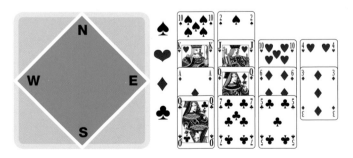

| West | North | East | South |
|------|-------|------|-------|
| 1♣ | 3♠ | Dble | |

At this level West will quite often pass the double for penalties. That is because it may be easier to score five or six tricks in defence, rather than make a contract at the four-level with no particularly good fit.

## Responder has a long suit

When you play negative doubles, the responder has two ways of bidding a new suit. Look at these two sequences, where East holds length in hearts:

**1**

| West | North | East | South |
|------|-------|------|-------|
| 1♠ | 2♣ | Dble | Pass |
| 2♦ | Pass | 2♥ | |

**2**

| West | North | East | South |
|------|-------|------|-------|
| 1♠ | 2♣ | 2♥ | |
| | | | |

In sequence (1) responder begins with a negative double and then introduces his long suit on the next round. In (2) he bids his long suit directly instead. It makes good sense to differentiate between these sequences in terms of strength. Most players treat sequence (2) as forcing, showing a strong hand with responder, and sequence (1) as non-forcing. Some players use the sequences the other way round, however, and it is something you should discuss with your partner.

## The opener re-opens with a double

When the double of an overcall is played for take-out, responder has to pass when he has a strong holding in the opponent's suit and would like to have doubled for penalties. The penalty will often return to the fold because his partner will re-open with a take-out double most of the time:

**Above:** Weak with hearts. On this type of hand you will use sequence (1) or (2), according to the methods you have agreed with your partner.

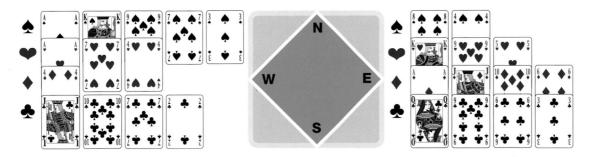

The opponents have stopped at the two-level, so the odds are good from West's point of view that his partner has several points and had to pass because he held length in diamonds. West doubles for take-out, mainly in the hope that partner can pass for penalties. As you see from this example, such a double does not promise any extra values with the opening bidder.

| West | North | East | South |
|------|-------|------|-------|
| 1♠ | 2♦ | Pass | Pass |
| Dble | End | | |

---

### APPEAL COMMITTEES
♠ ♥ ♦ ♣

When a player does not agree with a ruling that has been given by a director in a major tournament, he has the option of appealing against it. Usually he is required to deposit a sum of money, which will be forfeited if the appeal is deemed to be frivolous. An "appeal panel" of strong players will then convene to discuss the matter. If you look at the bulletins published on some tournaments, you will find almost as much material on the result of appeals as on the actual deals themselves!

---

# RESPONSIVE AND COMPETITIVE DOUBLES

It is rarely advantageous to double the opponents at a low level when they have found a trump fit. In this section we will look at two situations in which the other side has found a fit and it is therefore best to play a double for take-out instead of for penalties.

### The responsive double

When an opening bid has been doubled for take-out and the next player raises to the two- or three-level, a double by the fourth player is also for take-out. It is known as a responsive double.

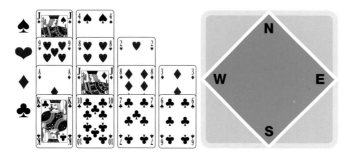

| West | North | East | South |
|------|-------|------|-------|
|      | 1♥    | Dble | 2♥    |
| Dble |       |      |       |

West can tell that his side holds at least half the points in the pack and therefore has no wish to allow the opponents to choose trumps at the two-level. Rather than guess which minor suit to bid, and perhaps end in a 4–3 fit, he makes a responsive double. Since East will almost always hold four spades for his take-out double of 1♥, West would tend to respond in spades if he held four of them. The responsive double on this auction is therefore likely to be based on a hand with the minor suits. Unless East has values to spare, he will rebid 3♣ or 3♦ at his next turn.

Many pairs play responsive doubles up to the level of 3♠ but it is something that you should agree with your partner. As we saw with the negative double, your partner is more likely to pass a double for penalties when the level of bidding is already quite high.

| West | North | East | South |
|------|-------|------|-------|
|      |       |      | 1♠    |
| Dble | 3♠    | Dble | Pass  |
| Pass | Pass  |      |       |

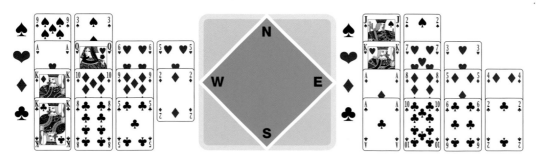

East's responsive double is for take-out but West cannot visualize a game their way, on his minimum double including a doubleton spade. He passes the double for penalties.

## The competitive double

Similarly, you can double for take-out when your partner has overcalled and the opponents have found a trump fit:

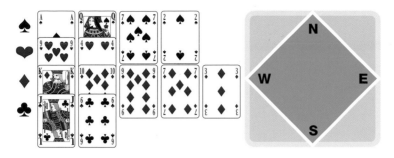

| West | North | East | South |
|------|-------|------|-------|
|      | 1♥    | 2♣   | 2♥    |
| Dble |       |      |       |

West's double is for take-out and is known as a competitive double. It suggests length in the unbid suits, spades and diamonds here, and a tolerance for partner's clubs, probably a doubleton. As before it would rarely be profitable to double for penalties at such a low level, once the opponents have found a trump fit.

Competitive doubles apply up to the level of 3♠, although you must agree this with your partner. As with the responsive double, partner will be more inclined to pass the double, the higher the level of the auction:

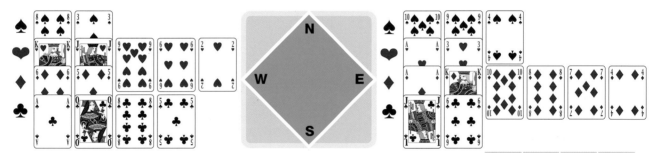

West's double is for take-out, a competitive double that shows values in hearts and clubs. East has no fit for either of these suits and decides that the best idea is to pass the double for penalties.

| West | North | East | South |
|------|-------|------|-------|
|      | 1♠    | 2♦   | 3♠    |
| Dble | Pass  | Pass | Pass  |

---

### THE VALUE OF CONVENTIONS
♠ ♥ ♦ ♣

Three famous Scientists vs Traditionalists matches have been played. One team was allowed to play unlimited conventions while the other could make only natural bids. In 1965, in New York, the Scientists (Roth/Stone, Mitchell/Stayman, Jordan/Robinson) beat the Traditionalists (Murray/Kehela, Becker/Hayden, Mathe/Schleifer) by 53 IMPs over 180 deals. In 1990, in London, the Scientists (Soloway/Goldman, Garozzo/Eisenberg) beat the Traditionalists (Zia/Chagas, Wolff/Forrester) by two sessions to one. In 1992, again in London, the Scientists (Hamman/Wolff, Rodwell/Meckstroth) beat Traditionalists (Chagas/Branco, Forrester/Robson) by 70 IMPs over 128 deals, winning a prize of $50,000.

**Above:** Jeff Meckstroth of the USA, a multiple world champion.

# SACRIFICING

Suppose your opponents bid to 4♥, a contract that is destined to succeed. If they are vulnerable, they will pick up a score of +620. When you and your partner hold a spade fit, it may be worthwhile for you to contest with 4♠. Even if you go two down, this will cost you only 300 when non-vulnerable, or 500 when vulnerable. That is good business already. In addition, the opponents may see fit to bid 5♥. If that contract goes one down, you will have done very well. Bidding a contract that you expect to fail, in the hope that it will cost you less than the opponents' contract, is known as sacrificing.

## Sacrificing at the game-level

The most common arena for sacrificing is the game-level. Here is a typical sacrifice deal:

**Right:** East–West can make 4♥ so it is profitable for North–South to sacrifice in 4♠, where the penalty will be less than the value of a game by the opponents.

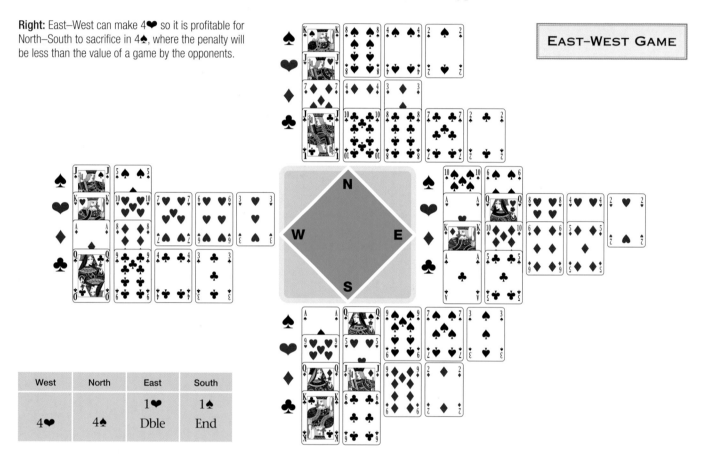

EAST–WEST GAME

| West | North | East | South |
|------|-------|------|-------|
|      |       | 1♥   | 1♠    |
| 4♥   | 4♠    | Dble | End   |

---

### TRUMP ECHO
♠ ♥ ♦ ♣

When defending at no-trumps, or following to a side suit in a suit contract, it is normal to play high–low to show an even number of cards. This is known as a "count signal". Somewhat strangely, it is widely agreed that a high–low signal in the trump suit has a quite different meaning. It shows precisely three trumps. Some players have the agreement that such a peter (or echo) also shows that you have the desire to score a ruff somewhere.

---

East–West bid to a game in hearts, a contract that will easily be made. Non-vulnerable against vulnerable, North decides to sacrifice in 4♠. He does not expect the contract to be made, but there is every chance that the cost will be less than that of the opponents' heart game.

So it proves. East–West are almost certain to find their diamond ruff but the penalty will still be only 300, much less than the 620 that the heart game would have provided. If either East or West had decided to bid 5♥, rather than accept a perhaps inadequate penalty from the spade game, this contract would have been defeated. With two spades in each hand, East-West were deterred from attempting a five-level contract.

## The five-level belongs to the opponents

A well-known guideline on sacrificing is that the five-level belongs to the opponents. In other words, if you have pushed the opponents to the five-level, it is rarely advantageous for you to bid five of a higher suit. Take your chance of beating their contract instead. For example, suppose that on the deal we have just seen East–West decided to advance to 5♥. It would be poor tactics for North–South to sacrifice again in 5♠. They should be content to have pushed their opponents to a possibly dangerous level.

Here is another typical sacrifice situation:

**Right:** When South sacrifices in 5♣, East-West should be wary of advancing to 5♥ and should therefore double.

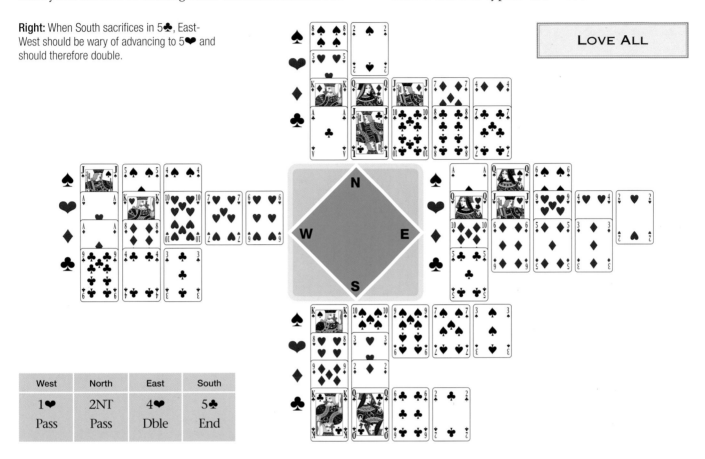

LOVE ALL

| West | North | East | South |
|------|-------|------|-------|
| 1♥   | 2NT   | 4♥   | 5♣    |
| Pass | Pass  | Dble | End   |

With the score at Love All, North enters the auction with an Unusual No-trump call to show length in both minor suits. South judges that the heart game is likely to succeed and sacrifices in 5♣. This runs to East, who takes note of the guideline "the five-level belongs to the opponents". Since the opponents have chosen to play in clubs, there is no reason for East to place his partner with a singleton diamond. There will be a loser or two in those suits. If the ♠K is missing, it is more likely that South will hold it than North (who has his length in the minor suits). So, East judges well to double. The cards lie well for North–South and the sacrifice goes only one down. Had East–West taken the push to 5♥, they would have gone down instead.

**Left:** South does not expect to make 5♣ but he expects it to cost less than a heart game made by the opponents.

# CHAPTER 2

# INTERMEDIATE CARD PLAY

It is time to see some important areas of card play that mainly involve looking at a contract as a whole, rather than considering only one particular suit. First you will see how to maintain communications between declarer's hand and the dummy – when one defender is "safe" and the other is "dangerous", you must plan to finesse or duck tricks into the safe hand. The important techniques of reversing the dummy and crossruffing are described next. Then you will see the various ways in which you can prevent the defenders from taking a ruff, also when you should delay drawing trumps because some other task is of higher priority. The idea of safety play is discussed and how you should calculate the best play with an unfamiliar card combination. Finally, you will see how a hold-up play can be useful in a suit contract as well as in no-trumps.

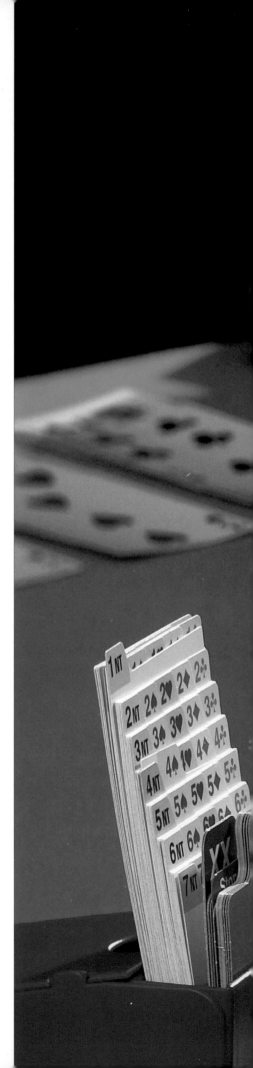

**Right:** Declarer has won the opening lead and is considering the best line of play. In a suit contract, the presence of a trump suit will offer you more options than in a no-trump contract.

# MAINTAINING COMMUNICATIONS

There is little point in creating an extra winner or two in the dummy if you have no entry with which to reach the dummy. An important part of planning a contract is to preserve the entries that you will need to get backwards and forwards between the two hands. The first deal involves two important techniques in this area:

**Right:** Declarer maintains communication to his diamond winners. Playing in 3NT, South has to employ two different techniques to set up and enjoy the diamond suit.

Hoping that your diamond suit will prove useful, you leap to 3NT on the South cards. The ♣Q is led and you must take some care with the entries to the South hand. The first step (often important) is to win the opening lead in the right hand. Here you must win with dummy's ace of clubs, preserving the club king as a later entry to your hand.

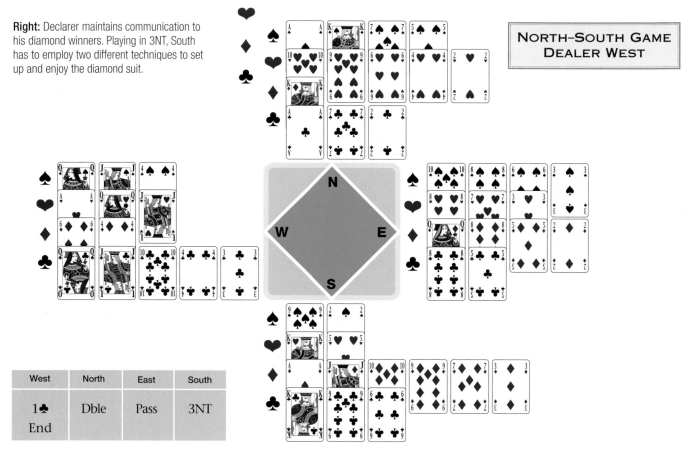

NORTH–SOUTH GAME
DEALER WEST

| West | North | East | South |
|------|-------|------|-------|
| 1♣ | Dble | Pass | 3NT |
| End | | | |

Suppose your next move is to cash the king of diamonds. You are most unlikely to make the contract. The only entry to your hand will be the king of clubs. If you cross to that card and play the ace of diamonds, you will make the contract only when the diamond queen happens to fall doubleton.

Instead, you should overtake the king of diamonds with the ace, thereby gaining an entry to the South hand. You then lead the jack of diamonds, forcing out East's queen. The game cannot then be defeated. The defenders can take at most one diamond and three hearts. When you regain the lead, you will have five diamonds and the two ace–kings in the black suits, giving you a total of nine.

**Right:** Declarer wins with a high card to preserve communications. A spade is led against 3NT and South must win with the ♠A to ensure that the ♠Q is preserved as an entry for dummy's club winners.

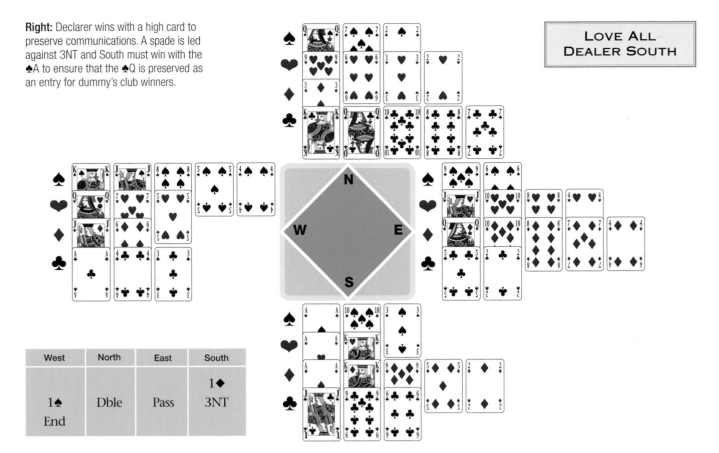

LOVE ALL
DEALER SOUTH

| West | North | East | South |
|------|-------|------|-------|
|      |       |      | 1♦    |
| 1♠   | Dble  | Pass | 3NT   |
| End  |       |      |       |

North's double on the first round is a "negative double", suggesting length in the unbid suits, hearts and clubs. West leads the ♠5 against the eventual contract of 3NT and, sitting South, you must consider the play carefully. You play low from dummy and East produces the ♠9. It may seem natural to win with the ♠10 but you will go down if you do so. When you play on clubs, West will hold up the ace until the third round. With ♠Q–7 facing ♠A–3 you will not have a spade entry to dummy. You will score only two club tricks and fall one trick short of your target.

To make the contract you must win the first trick with a higher card than is necessary. You capture East's ♠9 with the ace, even though your ♠10 would have been good enough to win the trick. When you play on clubs, West again holds up his ace until the third round. It will do him no good. Whatever suit he chooses to play next, you will be able to win and lead towards the ♠Q, establishing it as an entry for the two good clubs in the dummy. By disposing of the ♠A on the first round, you promote the ♠Q into a potential entry card.

**Left:** Helen Sobel and Charles Goren of the USA: one of the game's most famous partnerships.

# SAFETY PLAYS IN A SINGLE SUIT

The best way to play a suit often depends on how many tricks you need from it. Suppose you have to play this diamond suit:

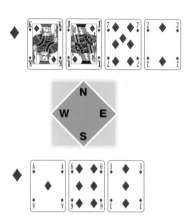

**Above:** The best play in this diamond suit depends on whether you need four diamond tricks or just three.

If you needed all four tricks from the suit, in order to make the contract, West would have to hold ◆Q–x–x. You would cash the ◆A and finesse the ◆J.

Now suppose that you need only three diamond tricks to make the contract. If you play the suit in the same way (◆A first, then finesse the ◆J), you will make the required three tricks when West holds the ◆Q, when diamonds break 3–3 and when East has a singleton ◆Q. You will fail in your objective when East holds ◆Q–x. When you need only three tricks, you should make the "safety play" of cashing the king and ace, then leading towards the jack on the third round. You will still make the required three tricks in the three situations just noted. You will succeed also when East holds ◆Q–x.

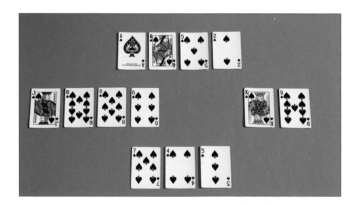

**Above:** Safety play. Needing only two tricks from the suit, you should duck a round, play the ♠A and then lead towards the ♠Q on the third round.

That's the idea of a safety play, then. You give yourself the maximum possible chance of making the number of tricks that you need. Suppose you are in 6♥ with this trump suit:

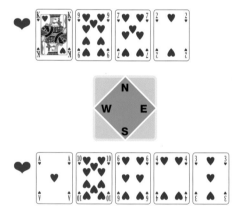

**Above:** If you can afford one loser in this suit, you must search for a safety play to avoid losing two tricks.

Let's say that there are no losers in the side suits. You are therefore looking for a safety play in the trump suit that will guard against two losers. If you play the ♥A first, you will lose two tricks when East began with ♥Q–J–x–x. Similarly, it is not safe to cash the ♥K first, in case West has all four missing trumps. The safe play is to lead towards dummy and play the ♥9. If West follows and East wins with the queen or jack, the suit must be breaking 3–1 at worst and you will lose only one trump trick. If West shows out on the first trump lead, your finesse of the ♥9 loses to one of East's honours, but you will later finesse the ♥10 to escape for one loser. (It would be just as good to lead towards the South hand on the first round, intending to finesse the ♥10.)

This is another combination that arises frequently:

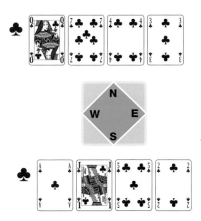

**Above:** If you need only three club tricks from this combination, you must seek a safety play that gives you the best chance of success.

When you need four club tricks, you play low to the jack in the hope that East holds a doubleton king. The king will then fall under the ace on the second round and dummy's ♣Q–7 will then score the remaining two tricks in the suit.

Suppose instead that you need only three club tricks. The safety play in that case is to cash the ♣A on the first round, thereby avoiding defeat when West holds a singleton ♣K.

We will look at one more suit combination, this time in the context of a complete deal.

West leads the ♥Q against 6♠ and your sole concern is to avoid two trump losers. If you were in the poor contract of 7♠, you would play the ace and king of trumps, hoping that the ♠Q fell. In the more sensible contract of 6♠ you can afford one trump loser. After winning the heart lead, you should cash the ♠A. You then cross to the South hand with a diamond and lead a low trump towards dummy on the second round.

When West follows with a low card, you will finesse dummy's ♠9. If the finesse loses to the ♠10, the suit will be breaking 3–2 and you are home. If instead East shows out, you will lose only one trump trick to West's remaining ♠Q–10.

When West holds ♠Q–10–8–2, as in the diagram, it will do him no good to "split his honours", playing the ♠10 on the second round. Your ♠9 and ♠J would then be equals against his ♠Q.

Suppose instead that West shows out on the second round of trumps. You then rise with dummy's king and lead towards the jack of trumps. This safety play guards against ♠Q–10–x–x in either defender's hand.

**Right:** A safety play in the trump suit. To avoid losing two trump tricks to a bad break, declarer must play the suit in a special way.

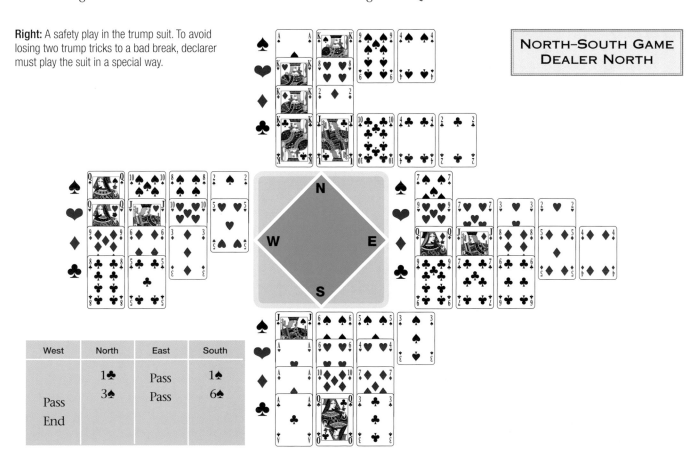

**NORTH–SOUTH GAME
DEALER NORTH**

| West | North | East | South |
|------|-------|------|-------|
|      | 1♣    | Pass | 1♠    |
|      | 3♠    | Pass | 6♠    |
| Pass |       |      |       |
| End  |       |      |       |

# FINESSING INTO THE SAFE HAND

It often happens that one defender's hand is "safe" and the other is "dangerous". For example, a defender may be dangerous because he has some winners to cash or can lead through an unprotected king. When you have a choice of finesses to take, you should usually finesse into the safe hand. Even if the finesse happens to fail, it will be the safe defender who gains the lead. The 3NT contract, shown below, is an example of that:

**Right:** Taking the right finesse first. When you may have to take two finesses (in clubs and diamonds here), it is usually best to finesse first into the safe hand.

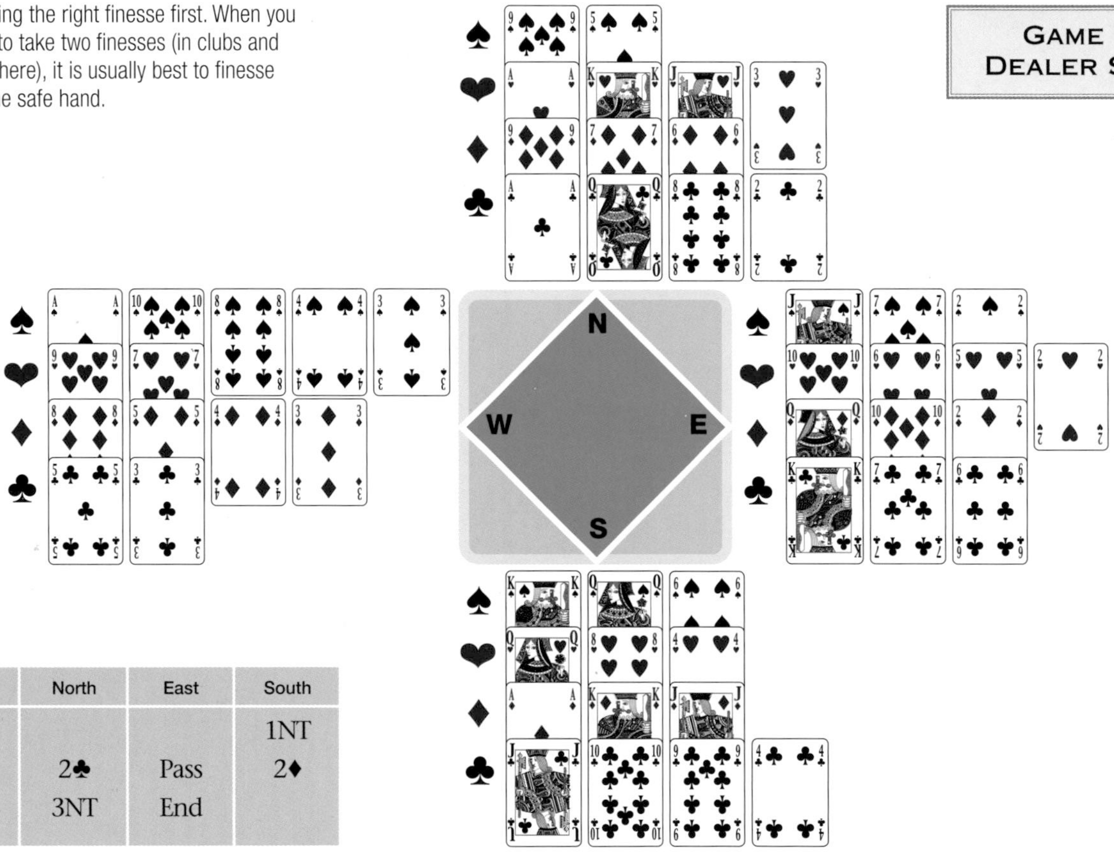

West leads the ♠4 and you win East's ♠J with the ♠K. You have eight top tricks and must decide which minor-suit finesse to take.

Suppose you run the ♣J at Trick 2. East will win with the ♣K and return a spade. The defenders will score four spades and one club, putting you one down. It was not a good way to play the contract because the club finesse was "into the dangerous hand". If it lost, East would damage you with a spade return.

> **GAME ALL**
> **DEALER SOUTH**

| West | North | East | South |
|------|-------|------|-------|
|      |       |      | 1NT   |
| Pass | 2♣    | Pass | 2♦    |
| Pass | 3NT   | End  |       |

---

## MOST COMMON HAND SHAPE

♠ ♥ ♦ ♣

Although 4–3–3–3 is the flattest possible shape for a bridge hand, it is only the fifth most common shape. Its frequency is 10.5 per cent. The most common shape is 4–4–3–2, which has a frequency of 21.5 per cent. It is followed by hands of 5–3–3–2 shape (15.5 per cent), 5–4–3–1 shape (12.9 per cent) and 5–4–2–2 shape (10.6 per cent).

A better idea is to cross to the ♥J and lead a diamond to the jack. This finesse is "into the safe hand". As it happens, the finesse succeeds and the contract is yours.

Suppose the diamond finesse were to lose, though. West could not profitably continue spades from his side of the table. (If he did play a spade, hoping that his partner held the ♠Q, he would give you your ninth trick.) If West played any suit other than a spade, you would win the trick and still be able to take the club finesse. By finessing into the safe hand you give yourself two chances instead of one.

Sometimes you have a two-way finesse for a missing queen. When you can afford to lose a trick in the suit and still emerge with enough tricks for your contract, it makes good sense to finesse into the safe hand. Look at the deal shown below.

West leads the ♥4 against 3NT and East plays the ♥Q. You hold up the ♥A until the third round, aiming to exhaust East of his cards in the suit. There are eight tricks on top and a ninth trick must come from the diamond suit. You can finesse either defender for the missing ♦Q and must decide which way to take the finesse.

You will score an extra trick from the diamond suit, even if the finesse fails. So you can afford the finesse to fail, provided the defenders do not cash enough tricks to beat you.

**Right:** Finessing into the safe hand. When you have a two-way finesse in a suit (diamonds, here) and can afford to lose a trick, finesse into the safe hand.

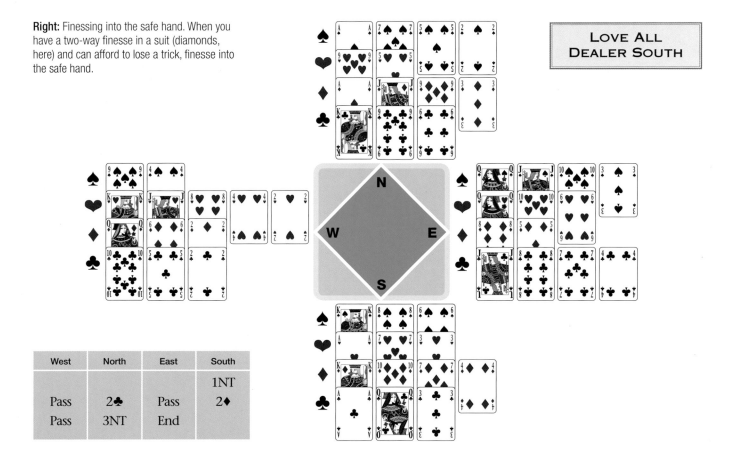

LOVE ALL
DEALER SOUTH

| West | North | East | South |
|------|-------|------|-------|
|      |       |      | 1NT   |
| Pass | 2♣    | Pass | 2♦    |
| Pass | 3NT   | End  |       |

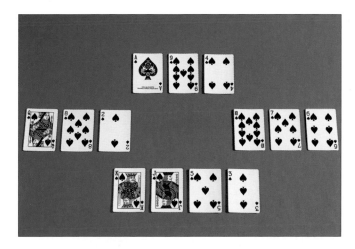

**Above:** Finessing into the safe hand. Suppose you only need three spade tricks. When West is the danger hand, it makes sense to lead low to the 9, losing a trick to the safe East hand.

Suppose you cross to the ♦A and run the ♦J on the way back, finessing East for the missing queen. This finesse is into the danger hand. If it loses, West will cash two hearts to beat the contract. Instead you should cash the ♦K and lead a low diamond towards dummy, intending to finesse West for the missing ♦Q. If the finesse loses to East, you will still make the contract. East has no hearts left and can do you no damage. (If he did have another heart, the suit would have broken 4–4 and would pose no problem.) As the cards lie in the diagram, the diamond finesse through West will succeed and you will end with an overtrick. The point to remember, though, is that by finessing into the safe hand you would make the contract whether the finesse succeeded or not.

# REVERSING THE DUMMY

Suppose you are playing in a spade contract with this trump holding:

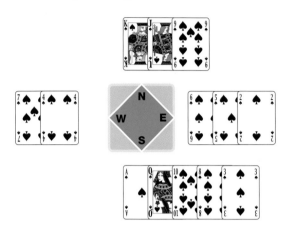

**Above:** If this is your trump suit, a ruff in the short-trump hand will give you an extra trick and a ruff in the long-trump hand will not.

You begin with five trump tricks and that will be the final number if you draw trumps near the start of the hand. Suppose instead that you take one ruff in the short-trump holding (the dummy). You will then make six trump tricks – five in your hand and one extra trick

**Right:** A typical dummy reversal. South increases the total number of trump tricks by ruffing three diamonds in the South hand.

from the ruff. If instead you ruffed something in the long trump hand, it would not give you an extra trick. You would still make just five trump tricks.

So, ruffing in the short trump hand gives you an extra trick; ruffing in the long trump hand does not. This is true in general, but if you take so many ruffs in the long trump hand that it becomes the short trump hand you can gain a trump trick. Look back at the spade position above. Take three ruffs in the South hand and you would score six trump tricks – three rounds of trumps in the North hand and three ruffs in the South hand. This is known as "reversing the dummy". Let's see an example featuring that very spade holding:

**NORTH–SOUTH GAME
DEALER SOUTH**

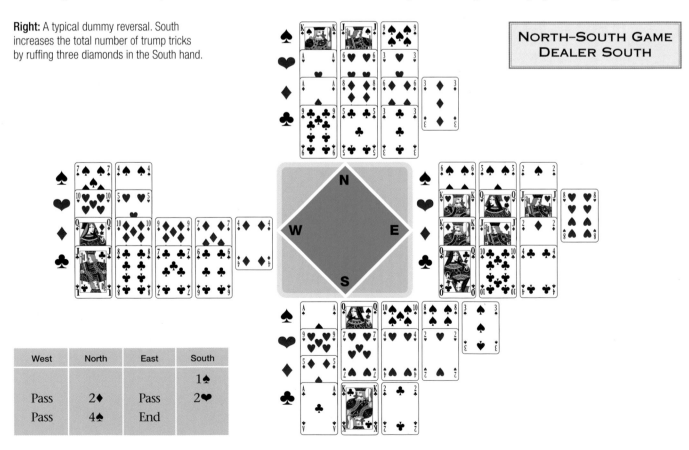

| West | North | East | South |
|------|-------|------|-------|
|      |       |      | 1♠    |
| Pass | 2♦    | Pass | 2♥    |
| Pass | 4♠    | End  |       |

West leads the ♠4 and you see that you have nine tricks on top. Without a trump lead, you could simply have given up two rounds of hearts and played to ruff the fourth round in dummy, if necessary. If you play that way now, though, the defenders will be able to remove dummy's trumps before you can take your heart ruff. A better idea is to reverse the dummy, aiming to ruff all three of dummy's diamond losers in the South hand.

You win the trump lead with the ♠9, cash the ♦A and ruff a diamond. You then play the ace and king of clubs, just in case a defender could discard his clubs as you ruff the diamonds. Returning to dummy with the ♥A, you ruff another diamond with the ♠A. You ruff with such a high trump because you want to lead the ♠10 next to dummy's ♠K. A third diamond ruff with the bare ♠Q gives you the first nine tricks and the ♠J is in the dummy, ready to give you a tenth trick.

It can also be worthwhile ruffing in your hand if this enables you to score the low trumps there. Had you attempted to draw trumps instead, these cards might have been losers.

Let's see a deal that illustrates this technique. Look at the 4♥ contract shown below, where the ace and king of trumps are accompanied by three low trumps.

West leads the ♦Q against your heart game and you win with dummy's ace. Even if trumps are breaking 3–2, you would still need some luck to avoid losing three clubs in addition to one trump. The best way to play the hand is to aim to make all five trumps in your hand (by ruffing three diamonds). Add in the five side-suit winners and that will come to ten. What is more, this line may well succeed when the trumps break 4–1.

Since entries to dummy are not plentiful, you should ruff a diamond at Trick 2. You then cash the ace–king of trumps, revealing that West began with four trumps. You continue with the king, queen and ace of spades, followed by a second diamond ruff. A club to the ace returns the lead to dummy and you ruff dummy's last diamond, both defenders following. Ten tricks are now before you. As you foresaw when you made your plan, you scored five side-suit winners and all five trumps in the South hand.

---

### MAKE A PLAN AT THE START
♠ ♥ ♦ ♣

It is not always right to draw trumps straight away. Always make a plan before starting to play the contract.

---

**Right:** Scoring the low trumps. Declarer reverses the dummy in order to make tricks with the low trumps in his hand.

LOVE ALL
DEALER SOUTH

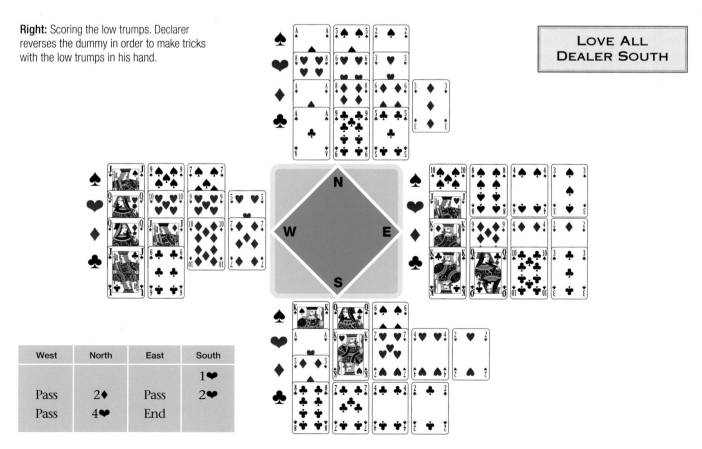

| West | North | East | South |
|------|-------|------|-------|
|      |       |      | 1♥    |
| Pass | 2♦    | Pass | 2♥    |
| Pass | 4♥    | End  |       |

# THE CROSSRUFF

Sometimes you are in a suit contract and both hands contain a singleton or void. In that case the best line of play may be to take several ruffs in each hand, never actually drawing trumps. The 4♠ contract shown below is a good example of this technique, which is known as the "crossruff":

**Right:** A typical crossruff. Declarer scores eight trump tricks by ruffing diamonds in dummy and hearts in his hand.

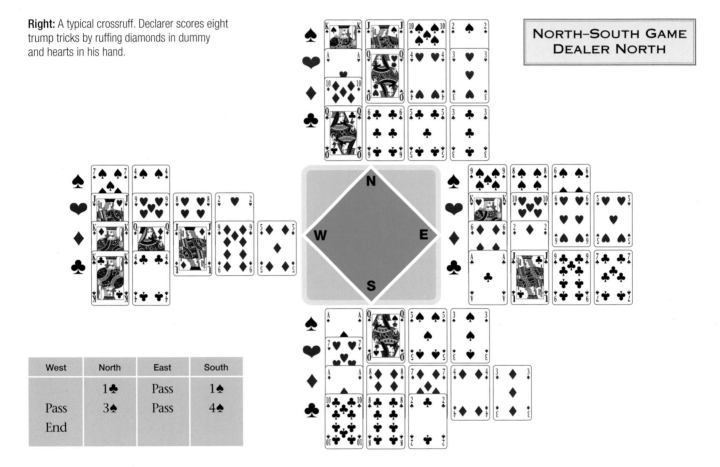

NORTH–SOUTH GAME
DEALER NORTH

| West | North | East | South |
|------|-------|------|-------|
|  | 1♣ | Pass | 1♠ |
| Pass | 3♠ | Pass | 4♠ |
| Pass | | | |
| End | | | |

West leads the ♦K against your game in spades. If you begin by drawing trumps, you will be well short of your target. Instead you should aim to make the two side-suit aces along with eight trump tricks. You must score all eight of your trumps separately, by taking ruffs in both hands.

You win the diamond lead with the ace and ruff a diamond with the ♠2. You cash dummy's ♥A and ruff a heart in the South hand, again with a low trump. When you ruff a second diamond East shows out. Since this ruff is with a high trump, East cannot overruff. You ruff a heart with the last low trump in the South hand and the contract is then safe. A diamond ruff, a heart ruff and a fourth diamond ruff, all with high trumps, bring your total to nine tricks and the ace of trumps will make it ten.

The important point to remember is that you take the early ruffs with low trumps, when the risk of an overruff is minimal. Later, you can ruff with high trumps and the defenders are powerless.

## QUALITIES NEEDED
♠ ♥ ♦ ♣

Many personal qualities bring a reward when it comes to playing bridge – patience, concentration and logical thought among them. Marshall Smith of the USA was once asked what qualities were required of a champion bridge player. Smith replied: "He needs the conceit of a peacock, the night habits of an owl, the rapacity of a crocodile, the sly inscrutability of a snake, the memory of an elephant, the boldness of a lion, the endurance of a bulldog and the killer instinct of a wolf."

On many hands you draw trumps first and then cash your side-suit winners. Since you never draw trumps when playing a crossruff, you should cash your side-suit winners at the beginning of the hand. If you fail to do this, the defenders may discard from those suits while you are crossruffing. They may then be able to ruff your winners. Look at this deal:

**Right:** Cashing the side-suit winners first. Declarer cashes the two winners in spades before embarking on the crossruff.

North's 4♦ rebid is a splinter bid, showing a sound raise to game in hearts with at most one diamond. South advances to a small slam, via Roman Key-card Blackwood and West leads the ♣5. As declarer, you can count four winners in the side suits. If you can add eight trump tricks, scored on a crossruff, this will bring the total to 12.

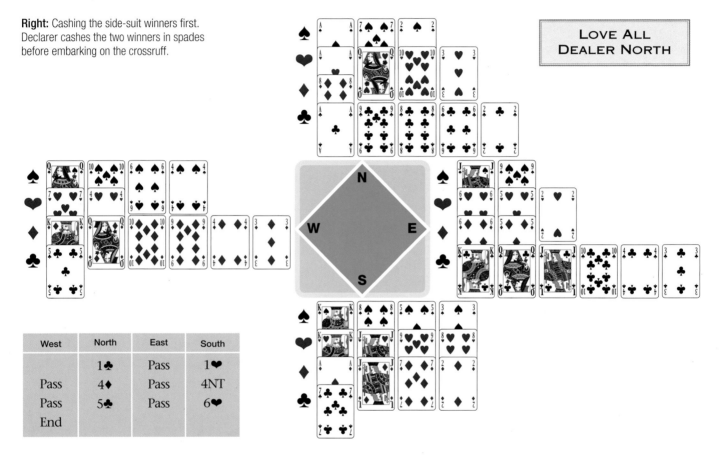

LOVE ALL
DEALER NORTH

| West | North | East | South |
|---|---|---|---|
|  | 1♣ | Pass | 1♥ |
| Pass | 4♦ | Pass | 4NT |
| Pass | 5♣ | Pass | 6♥ |
| End |  |  |  |

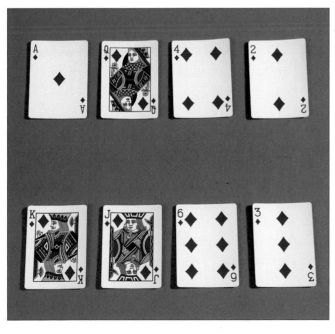

Suppose you embark on the crossruff immediately, ruffing clubs in your hand and diamonds in the dummy. When you take a second diamond ruff in dummy, East will discard one of his spades. It will no longer be possible for you to score two spade tricks, because East can now ruff the second round of the suit. The slam will go down.

To make the contract you must cash the ace and king of spades at the start, before the defenders have had an opportunity to discard any spades. Only then do you start the crossruff. Eight trump tricks will indeed come your way and the slam is made. In addition to the trump tricks, you will score two top spades and the minor-suit aces.

**Left:** Ruff low first. Suppose this is your trump suit and you need eight trump tricks on a crossruff. You would take the first four ruffs with low trumps. You would then continue with a "high crossruff", ruffing with the four honours.

# AVOIDING A RUFF

The most straightforward way to prevent the defenders from taking a ruff is to draw trumps. When you are missing the king or queen of trumps, you must be wary of taking an unnecessary trump finesse. If the finesse fails, the defender who wins the trick may be able to give his partner a ruff. You will often encounter deals like this:

**Right:** Avoiding a ruff by refusing a trump finesse. West leads his singleton diamond and declarer will go down if he takes a trump finesse.

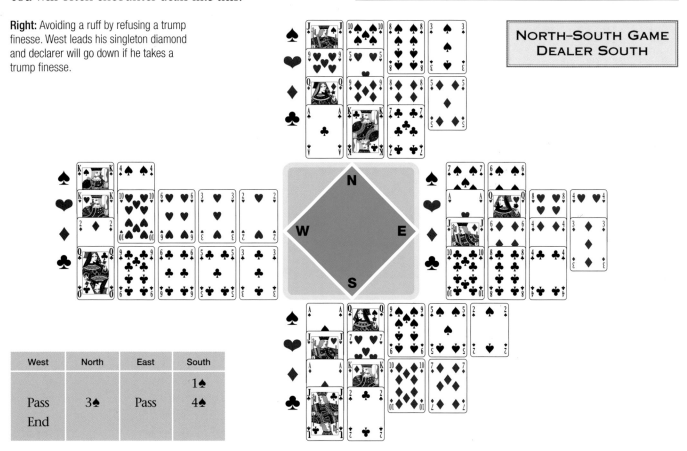

| | SUSPICIOUS LEAD ♠ ♥ ♦ ♣ | | |
|---|---|---|---|

When a defender leads a spot-card in a suit that you or the dummy has bid, you should suspect that it is a singleton and the defender is seeking a ruff.

**NORTH–SOUTH GAME DEALER SOUTH**

| West | North | East | South |
|------|-------|------|-------|
|      |       |      | 1♠    |
| Pass | 3♠    | Pass | 4♠    |
| End  |       |      |       |

West leads the ♦2. You play low from dummy and East plays the ♦J, won with your ace. It could hardly be more obvious that the opening lead is a singleton. Suppose you cross to dummy in clubs and run the ♠J. If the finesse loses, West can cross to his partner's hand with a heart and the ensuing diamond ruff will put the contract one down.

Since you have only two losers in the side suits, you can afford to lose a trump trick. You should therefore play ace and another trump. West wins the second round of trumps with the king and can no longer score a diamond ruff, because he has no trumps left. You will make the contract easily. This is another example of a safety play. You give up your best prospect

of picking up the trumps for no loser in exchange for maximizing your chance of making the contract.

You would make the same sort of play if dummy's trumps were ♠K–8–7–2 and your own trumps were ♠A–J–5–4. Suppose you took your best chance of playing the trumps for no loser, playing the ♠K and then finessing the ♠J. You would run the risk that West could win the second round from ♠Q–9–3 and cross to partner's hand with a heart to receive a diamond ruff.

To avoid such a fate, you would make the safety play of cashing the ace and king of trumps instead. You do not mind losing a trick to the queen of trumps. What you cannot afford is to lose two trump tricks – one to the queen, one to a ruff.

Similarly, when a ruff is threatened you may decide to forego a finesse in a side suit:

**Right:** Drawing trumps to avoid an adverse ruff. West leads ace and another heart against 4♠ and declarer must calculate whether to finesse the ♥J.

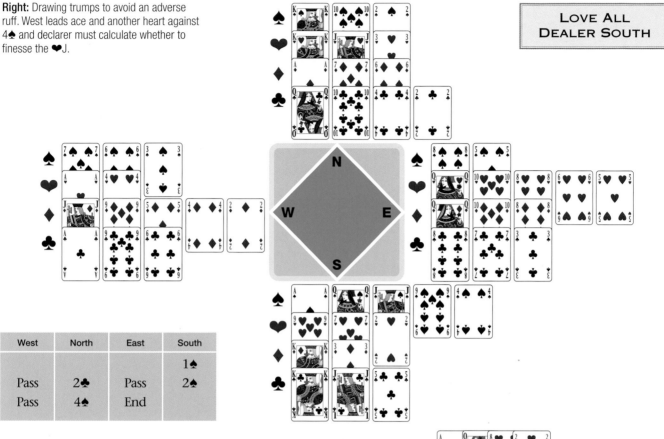

LOVE ALL
DEALER SOUTH

| West | North | East | South |
|------|-------|------|-------|
|      |       |      | 1♠    |
| Pass | 2♣    | Pass | 2♠    |
| Pass | 4♠    | End  |       |

Seeking a ruff, West leads the ♥A and continues with a second round of the suit. Suppose you see no harm in playing dummy's ♥J. East will win with the ♥Q and give West a heart ruff. You will go one down. Instead you should rise with dummy's ♥K. You can then draw trumps and will make the contract easily, losing just two hearts and one club.

There were two main reasons to play the ♥K at Trick 2. One is that players rarely lead from an ace–queen combination but often try their luck from a doubleton ace. The more compelling reason was that you would risk the contract by finessing the ♥J.

There are many similar positions. Suppose you reach a small slam in clubs, with a heart side suit as shown on the right.

West leads the ♥4 and you have no potential losers outside the heart suit. If you play a low card from dummy, you are running the risk that the opening lead is a singleton. In that case East will win with the ♥K and give partner a ruff. You should play safe for your slam. You rise with the ♥A, draw trumps and give the defenders a heart trick.

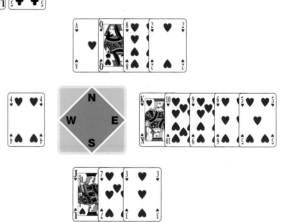

**Above:** When West leads the ♥4 against your small slam in clubs, you must be wary that the lead is a singleton.

---

### A LIKELY SINGLETON
### ♠ ♥ ♦ ♣

If a player opens with a pre-emptive bid of 3♠ and later leads a spot-card in a different suit, this is very likely to be a singleton, led in the hope of receiving a ruff. Unless his shape is precisely 7–2–2–2, a pre-empter will hold a singleton in his hand.

---

# THE HOLD-UP IN A SUIT CONTRACT

In an earlier section we looked at the very common play of holding up an ace in a no-trump contract. The purpose was to exhaust the holding of one defender. He then became "safe" and you could afford to lose the lead to him. Exactly the same play – holding up a stopper – can be effective in a suit contract too. Look at the deal shown below.

West leads the ♥K against 4♠. Even if trumps break 3–2, there are four potential losers: one spade, two hearts and one diamond. As declarer, you must seek to discard one of your heart losers on dummy's diamond suit.

Suppose you win the first trick with the ♥A and draw two rounds of trumps. You are over the first hurdle when the trump suit breaks 3–2. You will not make the contract, however. When you play a diamond, East will win with the ◆A and return his remaining heart, allowing West to score two heart tricks and beat the game.

The best chance of making the contract is to duck the first round of hearts. When West continues with a second round of the suit, you win with the ♥A and

lead the ◆K. You are now favoured with two strokes of luck. Firstly, it is East who holds the ◆A (if West held the card, he would be able to cash a heart winner). Secondly, East has no heart to play. Your hold-up on the first round of hearts did indeed exhaust his heart holding.

Let's say that East returns a club. You win the trick and play the queen and jack of diamonds, discarding your last heart. You will lose just one trump, one heart and one diamond. The game is yours.

As you may have noted, it would be a mistake to draw two rounds of trumps before leading the ◆K. East could then defeat you with a hold-up play of his own! By ducking the first round of diamonds and winning the second, he would leave you with no entry to reach the established ◆J in the dummy.

On the deal shown at the top of the next page you can diagnose that a hold-up at Trick 1 will work well. The opening lead marks East with the ♥K, so he will not be able to be able to continue the suit without allowing you to score both the the queen and ace.

**Right:** Holding up an ace in a suit contract. West leads the ♥K against the spade game and declarer must hold up for one round, to break the link between the defenders' hands.

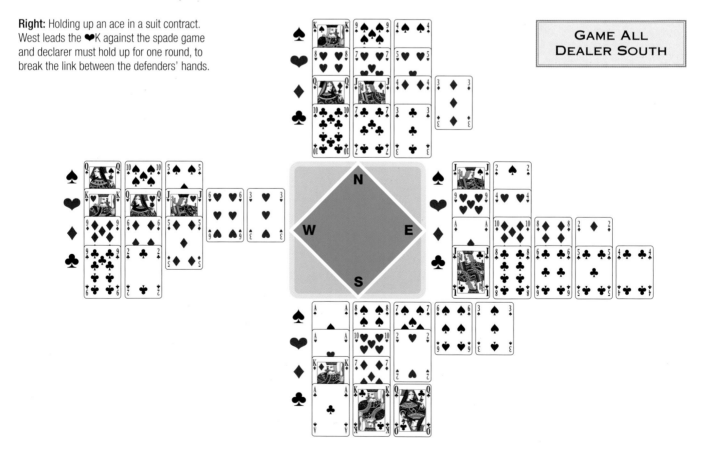

GAME ALL
DEALER SOUTH

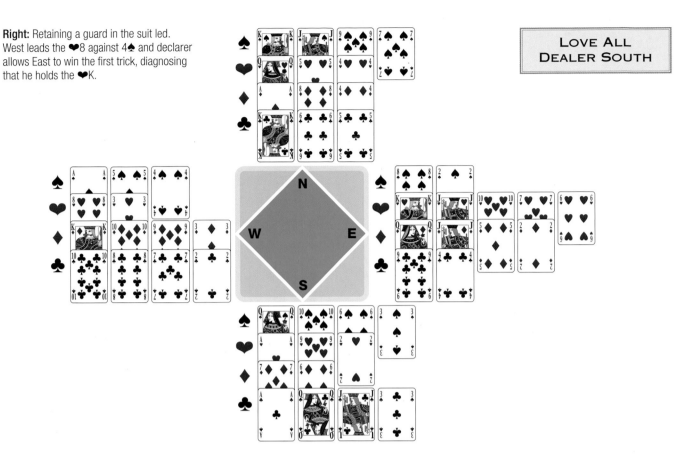

Right: Retaining a guard in the suit led. West leads the ♥8 against 4♠ and declarer allows East to win the first trick, diagnosing that he holds the ♥K.

West leads the ♥8 against 4♠. You play low from dummy and East plays the ♥10. You can see four potential losers: one trump, two hearts and one diamond. A heart can be discarded from dummy on the fourth club but the risk is that the defenders will claim their four tricks before you can take a discard.

The first task is to read the likely lie of the heart suit. West would not have led the ♥8 from ♥K–J–10–8, so the lead must be from spot cards, leaving East with the ♥K–J–10. The winning play is therefore to duck the first trick, allowing East's ♥10 to win. He cannot continue the suit safely because you would run a heart

return to dummy's queen. (You would then make the contract because, by good fortune, the ace of trumps lies with West, the defender who cannot deliver a heart ruff.)

Let's say that East senses this and switches to a diamond instead. You win with the ace and play a trump. When West takes the ace of trumps and plays another heart, you win with the ace, draw trumps and play four rounds of clubs, discarding dummy's last heart. You will then lose one trump, one heart and one diamond, making your game. Had you won the first round of hearts, the defenders would have scored two tricks in the suit when West won with the ♠A.

---

### PLAYING SPEED
♠ ♥ ♦ ♣

The normal rate of play in duplicate bridge events is eight hands per hour. Some hands take longer to bid and play than others, of course, and the players are expected to make up time by playing more quickly when they get behind on the clock. Fines can be administered for slow play, but it is often difficult to ascertain which pair was to blame.

Right: The 1973 Las Vegas Falls Nationals.

# WHEN TO DELAY DRAWING TRUMPS

When you are playing in a suit contract, the general rule is that you should draw trumps immediately unless there is a good reason to do something else first. The most common reason for playing a side suit instead is that you need to take a quick discard, or perhaps establish a discard. Look at this deal:

**Right:** Setting up a discard before drawing trumps. If declarer draws trumps immediately, rather than setting up a discard on the clubs, his 4♠ contract will go down.

West leads the ♦Q against your spade game. There are three aces to be lost, so you cannot afford a further loser in the diamond suit. Suppose you win the opening lead and play a trump immediately. East will win with the ace of trumps and clear the diamond suit. With no way to avoid a diamond loser, you will go one down.

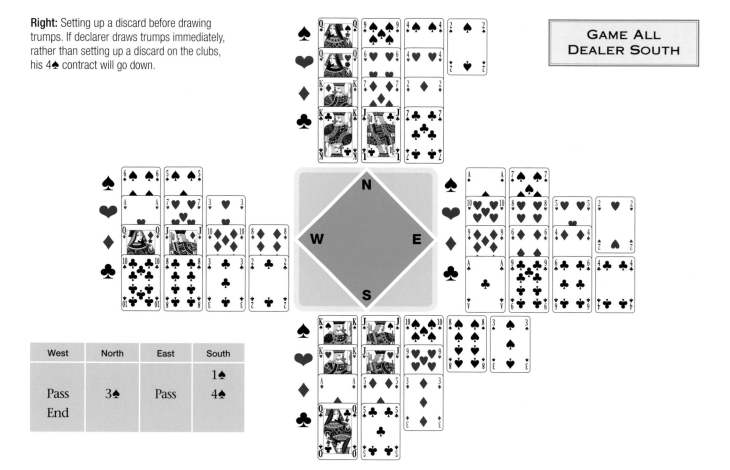

GAME ALL
DEALER SOUTH

| West | North | East | South |
|------|-------|------|-------|
|      |       |      | 1♠    |
| Pass | 3♠    | Pass | 4♠    |
| End  |       |      |       |

To make the contract you must delay drawing trumps, setting up a discard on the club suit instead. You win the diamond lead with the ♦A, preserving the ♦K as a later entry to dummy and lead the ♣Q. Let's say that East holds up the ♣A for one round. When you continue with a club to the king, East wins with the ace and returns a diamond. Now you reap the benefit of winning the first round of diamonds in your hand. You win with the ♦K and discard your diamond loser on the established ♣J. You can then play trumps safely and will make the game for the loss of just three aces.

Another reason to delay drawing trumps is when you need to make good use of the trump entries to dummy. This is most often the case when dummy contains a long side suit that you need to establish. That is the situation on the next deal:

**Right:** Establishing a side suit before drawing trumps. Declarer delays drawing trumps, so he can use the trump ace as an entry to establish dummy's diamond suit.

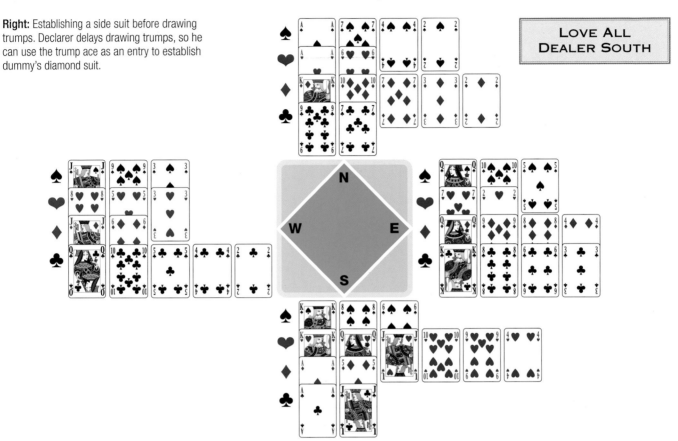

LOVE ALL
DEALER SOUTH

West leads the ♣4 against 6♥ and you win East's ♣K with the ♣A. You have 11 top tricks and must seek to establish at least one extra trick from dummy's diamond suit. Suppose your first move is to draw trumps. You continue with the ace and king of diamonds and then ruff a third round of diamonds. All would be well if diamonds divided 3–3. When they break 4–2, as in the diagram, you will go down. You have only one entry left to the dummy (the ♠A) and the diamonds are not yet established.

You need to use the ♥A as an extra entry to the dummy. After winning the club lead, you play the ace and king of diamonds. You ruff a third round of diamonds with the ♥K (to avoid a possible overruff). Next you cross to the ♥A and ruff a diamond with the ♥Q. You can then draw the outstanding trumps and cross to the ♠A to score the established ♦10.

To make such a contract, you must form a plan right at the start. If you make the mistake of drawing trumps first, it will be too late for any planning. You need to establish the diamonds. This will require two ruffs when the defenders' cards divide 4–2, in which case you will need to use the ♥A as an entry to take the second ruff.

**Above:** Declarer sees that he cannot afford to draw trumps straightaway.

# DUCKING INTO THE SAFE HAND

To establish a suit, it is often necessary to duck a round – in other words to let the defenders win an early trick in the suit. When one of the defenders is "safe" and the other is "dangerous", you must try to duck a trick into the safe hand. Here is a straightforward example of the play:

### NUMBER OF BRIDGE HANDS
♠ ♥ ♦ ♣

There are 635,013,559,600 different bridge hands that can be dealt.

**Right:** Establishing a suit by ducking into the safe hand. Declarer holds up the ♠A twice and then sets up the diamond suit by ducking a round into the safe East hand.

NORTH-SOUTH GAME
DEALER SOUTH

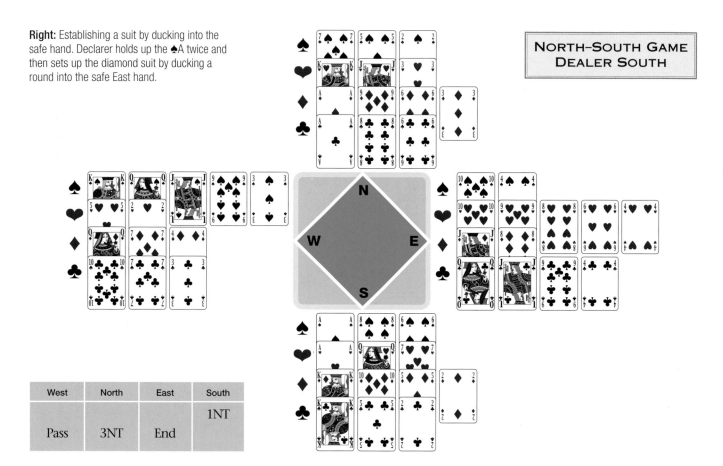

| West | North | East | South |
|------|-------|------|-------|
|      |       |      | 1NT   |
| Pass | 3NT   | End  |       |

West leads the ♠K against 3NT. Since you are well protected in the other three suits, nothing can be lost by holding up the ♠A until the third round. East discards a heart on the third round of spades. You have eight tricks on top and must try to develop a ninth trick from the diamond suit. This must be done without allowing West to gain the lead.

Suppose you play the ace and king of diamonds and concede a third round of the suit. All would be well if East began with three diamonds. He would win the third round and would have no spade to play. If the cards lie as in the diagram, however, you will go down. West will win the third diamond and cash two spades to put you one down.

You should lead the ♦2 from the South hand and play the ♦9 from dummy. You are ducking the trick into the safe hand. East wins with ♦J and has no spade to play. You win his return in some other suit and cash a total of nine tricks to make the game. Had you played ace, king, and another diamond instead, West would have won the third round of the suit and beaten the contract by cashing two more spade tricks.

Sometimes you duck a round of a suit as a safety play, to guard against a bad break. By ducking into the safe hand, you avoid the risk that the suit will break badly and you would otherwise have to lose a trick to the danger hand. That is the situation on the deal shown opposite.

West leads the ♥4 against 3NT and you win East's ♥Q with the ♥K. (If instead you were to allow the ♥Q to win, East would continue with a second heart and West would hold up his ♥A to maintain communication between the defenders.) You have eight tricks on top and need to develop a ninth trick from the diamonds. If the suit divided 3–3, you would have two extra diamond tricks ready to take, simply by playing the suit from the top. If you play that way here, East will win the fourth diamond and beat you by returning a heart through your ♥J–7. To make the contract even when East holds four diamonds, you need to duck a diamond trick into the safe (West) hand.

At Trick 2 you cross to the ♠A. You then lead the ♦5. When East follows with a low spot-card you cover with the ♦8, ducking a diamond trick into the safe hand. West wins with the ♦10 but cannot continue hearts successfully from his side of the table. If he switches to a club, you will rise with dummy's ♣A. You then play a diamond to the queen and return to dummy with the ♠K to score three more diamond tricks for the contract.

By making this safety play, ducking a round of diamonds, you would score only four diamond tricks instead of five when the suit divided 3–3. The potential loss of an overtrick is a small premium to pay for making the game when diamonds break 4–2.

If East began with ♦J–10–4–2 he would (if awake) play one of his honours on the first round, to prevent you ducking the trick into the safe hand. The contract could not then be made when the heart suit lies as in the diagram.

**Right:** Ducking into the safe hand in case a suit breaks badly. Declarer ducks a diamond into the safe (West) hand, so that he can establish the suit when the defenders' cards break 4–2.

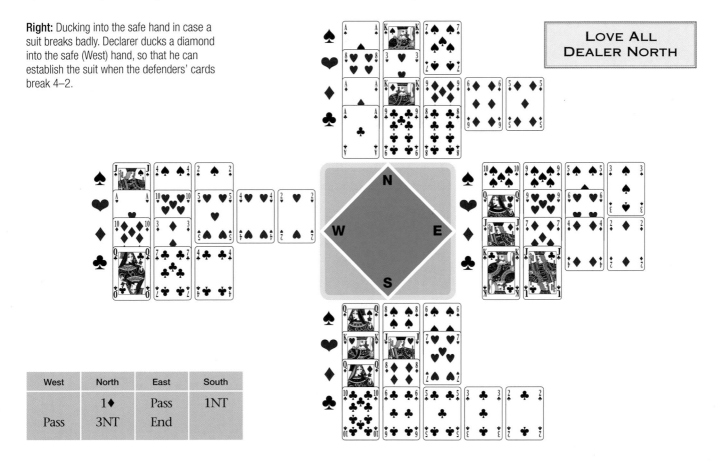

LOVE ALL
DEALER NORTH

| West | North | East | South |
|------|-------|------|-------|
|      | 1♦    | Pass | 1NT   |
| Pass | 3NT   | End  |       |

---

### PUT THE SAFE HAND ON LEAD
♠ ♥ ♦ ♣

Suppose you are in a suit contract, with a side suit of ♦K–8–2 in dummy and a singleton ♦5 in your hand. When West leads the ♦Q, it is obvious that East holds the ♦A. If you think that West could make a damaging play at Trick 2, you should cover with the ♦K, to make sure that East wins the first trick. Otherwise you should duck.

# Chapter 3

# Intermediate defence

It is a familiar concept to plan the play of a hand when you are the declarer. It can be just as important to plan the defence of a contract and here you will see how you can do this, both in a suit contract and in no-trumps. You will see also how dangerous it can be to defend too actively by attacking new suits. This is all too likely to give away an unnecessary trick. You need to study all the available evidence before deciding whether to be active or passive with your defence. One of the most difficult areas of defence, contrary to what some players will tell you, is whether to cover an honour card that has been led. You need to make such decisions in advance, so that you do not give information away by thinking about your play when a particular card is led. Finally the important topic of retaining the right cards in defence will be addressed.

**Right:** The opponents' bidding will often give you a good idea what the general line of defence should be. The opening lead represents an important part of the defence.

# PLANNING THE DEFENCE IN A SUIT CONTRACT

To defend accurately is not easy. You must think clearly and, above all, you must count. You count the tricks available to the defenders and to declarer. You count the points shown by declarer and by your partner. You also count the distribution of the suits, hoping to end with a complete count of the hand. If you think this sounds rather like hard work, you are right. It is the price that has to be paid in order to become a top-class defender.

## Counting tricks for the defence

On the following deal, East's defence is dictated by counting the tricks that he can see for the defenders.

Sitting East, you see partner lead the ♣2. You win with the ♣A and pause to plan the defence. It is unlikely that the defence will score any tricks from the major suits. You must therefore hope for four tricks from the minors. You can score three club tricks only if West has led specifically from ♣K–J–2, which is not a big chance. It is more likely that you can score two club tricks and two diamond tricks. So, you should switch to the ♦2 at Trick 2. As the cards lie, declarer will rise with the ♦K and West will score tricks with the ace and jack of diamonds. The ♣K will then be the setting trick. As you see, a wooden club return at Trick 2 would have allowed the contract to make. West would win with the club king but could not attack diamonds effectively from his side of the table.

The recommended defence might succeed also when declarer held ♦K–J–x. He would then have to guess which diamond honour to play. If he decided to rise with the ♦K, he would again lose four tricks in the minors and go one down.

**Right:** Counting the defensive tricks. By counting the tricks available to the defence, East makes the right play on the second trick.

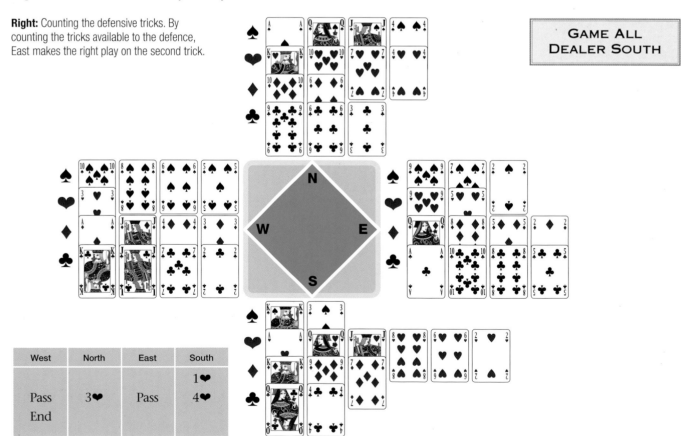

**GAME ALL
DEALER SOUTH**

| West | North | East | South |
|------|-------|------|-------|
|      |       |      | 1♥    |
| Pass | 3♥    | Pass | 4♥    |
| End  |       |      |       |

On the next deal, counting defensive tricks allows East to judge that he should delay giving partner a ruff.

**Right:** Delaying a defensive ruff. West leads his singleton club against 4♠. By counting the defensive tricks, East calculates that it is not right to give partner a ruff at the second trick.

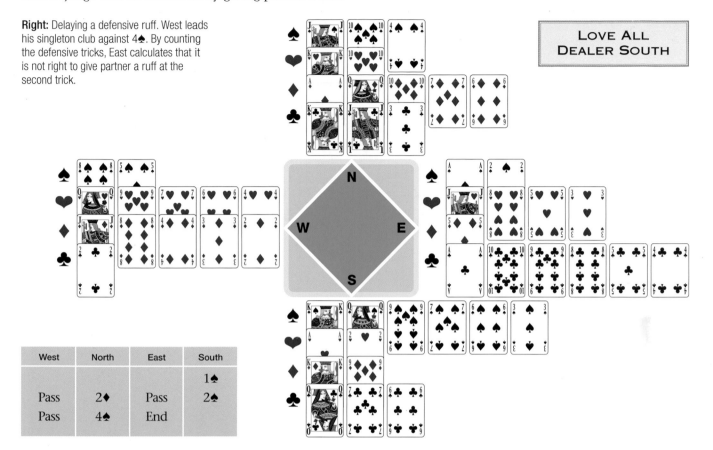

LOVE ALL
DEALER SOUTH

| West | North | East | South |
|------|-------|------|-------|
|      |       |      | 1♠    |
| Pass | 2♦    | Pass | 2♠    |
| Pass | 4♠    | End  |       |

You hold the East cards. Your partner leads the ♣2 and you win with the ♣A. The odds are high that the opening lead is a singleton. Suppose you return a club immediately, however, giving partner a ruff. You must ask yourself how many tricks the defenders will score. Ace of clubs, a club ruff and the ace of trumps. That is three tricks. If partner started with three trumps, you will be able to give him a second club ruff but that is no certainty. As the cards lie, West will not be able to score a second club ruff and the game will be made.

Instead of returning a club without thought, you should pause to make a plan for the defence. You know that you can give partner the lead with a club ruff. Since you hold the ace of trumps, there is no need to deliver the ruff immediately. To ensure that you score a ruff too, you must switch to your singleton diamond at Trick 2. Declarer wins the trick in the dummy and leads a trump. You rise with the ace of trumps and only now give your partner a club ruff. He returns a diamond, allowing you to ruff, and the game goes one down.

---

### GRAND MASTER
♠ ♥ ♦ ♣

Rixi Markus (1910–92) was the first woman to become a Grand Master under the World Bridge Federation ranking scheme. Rixi was a tigress at the table but very charming once the game was over. Her most famous partnership was with Fritzi Gordon (1916–92). Together they won two World Pairs Olympiads, a World Teams Olympiad, and eight European championships.

**Above:** Rixi Markus

**Above:** Fritzi Gordon

## Counting tricks for the declarer

On many deals you can reach the right decision in defence by counting the tricks that are available for declarer. Take the East cards on the deal below.

West leads the ♦Q, which marks declarer with the ♦K. If he holds six solid trumps, he will make the game easily because there is no way that you can score three quick heart tricks, however the cards lie. You must therefore assume that West holds a trump trick.

Suppose you return the ♦7 at Trick 2, aiming to knock out South's ♦K and establish a diamond trick for the defence. It is quite likely then that declarer will score five trump tricks, four clubs and the ♦K.

**Right:** Diagnosing a switch by counting declarer's tricks. West leads the ♦Q against the spade game. By counting the number of tricks available to declarer, East sees the need to switch to hearts.

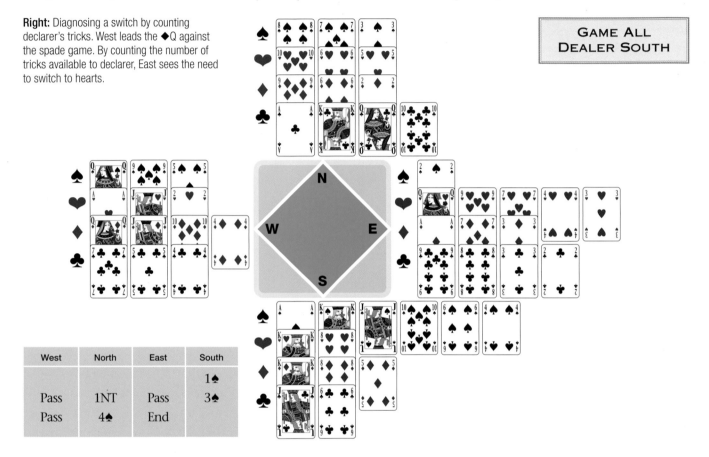

GAME ALL
DEALER SOUTH

| West | North | East | South |
|------|-------|------|-------|
|      |       |      | 1♠    |
| Pass | 1NT   | Pass | 3♠    |
| Pass | 4♠    | End  |       |

With discards threatened on dummy's clubs, you should switch to the ♥4 at Trick 2, claiming whatever tricks may be available there. As the cards lie, your partner will score two heart tricks and his eventual trump trick will put the game one down.

As you see, a diamond return would have allowed the game to make. Declarer would win with the ♦K, draw two rounds of trumps and turn to the club suit. The diamond loser would be thrown on the third club and one of the heart losers on the fourth club. It would make no difference whether or not West chose to ruff this trick with the ♠Q. Declarer would lose only one trump, one diamond and one heart.

When you can see that declarer has quick discards available, you must switch immediately to the side suit where you may have some quick winners to take.

Here is another deal where you can benefit from counting declarer's tricks. Again you are in the East seat.

West leads the ♣J and declarer plays low from dummy. You must now decide whether to play your ♣A. It may seem attractive to play low, in order to avoid giving declarer two club tricks when he began with ♣Q–x–x. Before doing so, you should check how many tricks declarer will have after such a start to the defence. He will almost certainly have six trump tricks. To this you must add two diamond tricks, once the ♦A is dislodged, one club trick with the queen and one heart trick. That is a total of ten, so you can expect the contract to succeed if you play low at Trick 1.

To beat the contract you need to score the minor-suit aces and two heart tricks. To allow this to happen, you must rise with the ♣A at Trick 1 and then switch to the ♥J, knocking out one of the dummy's heart stoppers. Declarer has no way to counter such a lively defence. No doubt he will draw trumps and play a diamond towards the dummy. Your partner will rise with the ♦A and play a second round of hearts, giving you two tricks in the suit. The game then goes one down.

You might achieve the same result by counting the possible tricks for the defence. Since there is only one likely trick in the black suits (the ♣A), you will need the ♦A and two heart tricks to beat the contract.

If you watched such a defence in a major championship, you might gasp in amazement. As you see, you can calculate quite logically that it is the only real chance to beat the contract. You must attack the heart suit before the ♦A is removed.

**Right:** Visualizing the defensive tricks. West leads the ♣J against the spade game and East must count declarer's tricks to diagnose the winning defence.

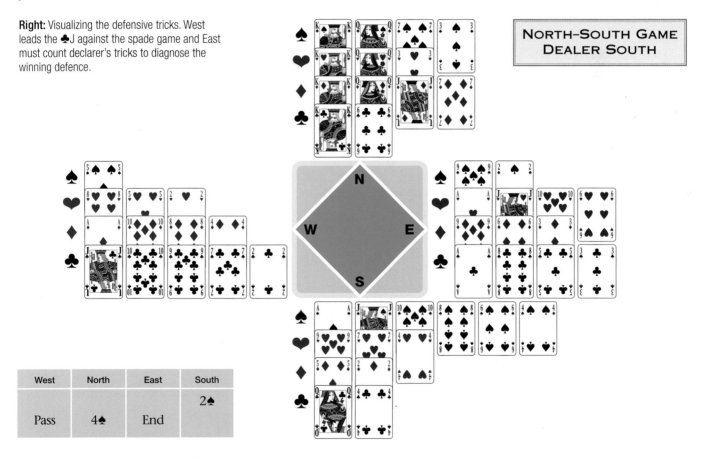

NORTH-SOUTH GAME
DEALER SOUTH

| West | North | East | South |
|------|-------|------|-------|
|      |       |      | 2♠    |
| Pass | 4♠    | End  |       |

---

### THE QUESTION TO ASK
♠ ♥ ♦ ♣

When defending, do not restrict yourself to automatic plays such as "leading up to weakness" and "returning partner's suit". Instead, ask yourself the question: "How can this contract be defeated?" If you need partner to hold a particular card, such as an ace, continue the defence on the assumption that he holds this card.

# PLANNING THE DEFENCE IN NO-TRUMPS

Defending at no-trumps tends to be easier than in a suit contract. With the elements of ruffing and trump control not present, you can concentrate on communications and on setting up the tricks that you need to beat the contract. When you are sitting over the dummy, the most important decision is often whether to continue partner's suit or to switch elsewhere. By counting declarer's potential tricks, you may find a clear indication of the best chance.

## Counting tricks for the declarer

Take the East cards on this deal and see if you would have come to the right "continue or switch?" decision.

West leads the ♥5 against 3NT and your jack is won by South's ace. Declarer leads the ♣Q at Trick 2, West following with the ♣7. You win with the king and pause for a moment to decide what to do next. Is it possible that your partner led from ♥K–Q–x–x–x and that the heart suit is now ready to run? No, because if declarer had started with ♥A–x–x, he would have held up the ace

for two rounds to exhaust you of your holding in the suit. So, declarer began with ♥A–K–x. (He should have won the first trick with the ♥K, to make this less obvious to you, but not all declarers know that.)

It may seem natural to knock out declarer's last heart stopper, nevertheless. Before doing this, you should count the tricks that would then be at declarer's disposal. He would have three club tricks, two hearts and almost certainly four diamond tricks. That is a total of nine. So, you cannot afford to continue with partner's suit. You must hope to score four quick tricks elsewhere and this can be achieved only in the spade suit. Switch to the ♠Q in the hope that partner holds ♠A–10–x–x. When the cards lie as in the diagram you will beat the contract.

Defenders who follow simple rules such as "Always return partner's suit" would allow this contract to be made. Good bridge is rarely a question of following this or that rule. In defence, you must think clearly whether a particular defence has a chance of beating the contract.

**Right:** Counting declarer's tricks. By counting the tricks available to declarer, East diagnoses the right switch when he gains the lead.

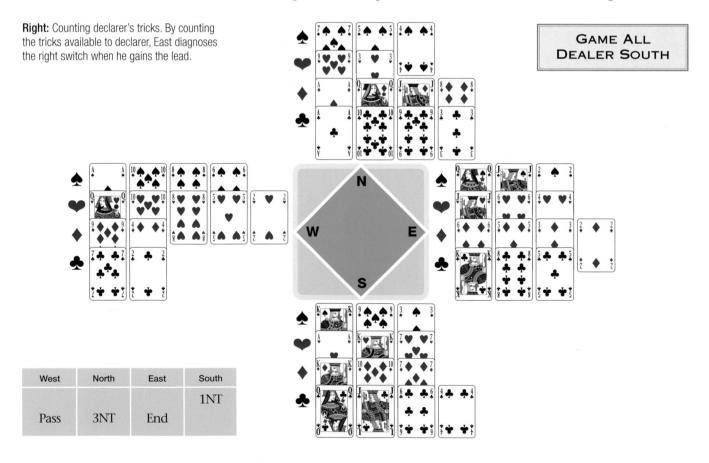

GAME ALL
DEALER SOUTH

| West | North | East | South |
|------|-------|------|-------|
|      |       |      | 1NT   |
| Pass | 3NT   | End  |       |

**Above:** When the ♥J is won with the ♥A, the defender places declarer with ♥A–K.

## Reading the opening lead

A clever gadget known as "The Rule of Eleven" will often assist you in reading the lie of the suit that partner has chosen to lead. When partner has made a fourth-best lead from a suit headed by an honour, you subtract the spot-card that he has led from 11. The answer will give you the number of higher cards that are held by the other three hands. Suppose partner has led the ♥6 and the heart suit lies as shown below.

You are sitting East and your ♥Q is won by declarer's ♥K. By applying the Rule of Eleven, you can tell that the North, East and South hands contain

between them five cards higher than the ♥6. (You subtract 6 from 11, getting 5 as the answer.) You can see four of these cards in your own hand and the dummy (the queen, ten nine and seven of the suit). So the ♥K is the only high card that declarer holds in the suit. The defenders' hearts are ready to run. Such knowledge might enable you to rise immediately with an ace in a different suit, switching back to hearts.

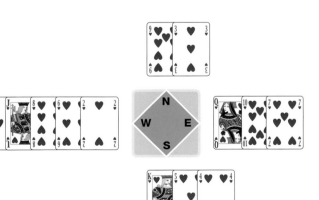

**Above:** Rule of Eleven. By applying the Rule of Eleven to West's opening lead of the ♥6, East can determine the lie of the heart suit.

Let's see a complete deal featuring that heart suit. Take the East cards and plan your defence to this 3NT contract:

**Right:** Rule of Eleven. West leads the ♥6 to East's ♥Q and South's ♥K. East applies the Rule of Eleven to determine his future defence.

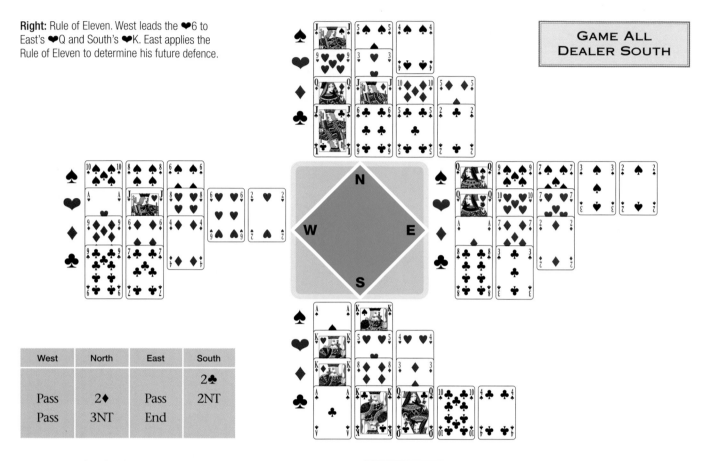

GAME ALL
DEALER SOUTH

| West | North | East | South |
|------|-------|------|-------|
|      |       |      | 2♣    |
| Pass | 2♦    | Pass | 2NT   |
| Pass | 3NT   | End  |       |

West leads the ♥6 against South's 3NT contract and declarer wins your queen with the king. At Trick 2 he leads the ♦K and you must think carefully how to defend. If you consider the diamond suit in isolation, you might well decide to hold up the ♦A for a round or two, hoping to prevent declarer from enjoying dummy's diamond winners. Such a plan will not work well here, though. If declarer is allowed to make even one diamond trick, he will unveil seven more tricks in the black suits and make his contract.

To beat 3NT, you must win the very first diamond trick and return a heart. How can you be sure that this is the right thing to do? The Rule of Eleven tells you that declarer has no stopper remaining in hearts. There is also a good chance that your partner began with a five-card heart suit because he led the ♥6 and the five, four and two of the suit are missing. Unless declarer began with specifically ♥K–5–4–2, your partner started with at least five hearts and a heart switch will be successful. So, do not follow some

> ### ROUNDED AND POINTED
> ♠ ♥ ♦ ♣
> Clubs and spades are known as the "black suits"; clubs and diamonds are known as the "minor suits". What could clubs and hearts be called? Since both symbols are rounded at the top, they became known as the "rounded suits". Similarly, diamonds and spades are known as the "pointed suits".

general rule about "holding up an ace to kill the dummy". Take the ♦A immediately and return the ♥10. Your partner will score four tricks in the suit to defeat the contract.

Sometimes the Rule of Eleven will tell you that partner's lead cannot be a fourth-best card, so he has led his second-best card from a weak suit. In that case it will usually pay you to abandon the suit that has been led and to seek tricks from elsewhere. A high-card lead is a warning that tricks are unavailable from that source.

**Right:** Diagnosing that the lead is from a weak suit. East calculates that the ♠7 lead must be from a weak suit and defends accordingly, switching to hearts.

| West | North | East | South |
|------|-------|------|-------|
|      |       |      | 1NT   |
| Pass | 3NT   | End  |       |

South opens a 15–17 point 1NT and is raised to game. West leads the ♠7 against this contract and the ♠10 is played from dummy. Sitting East, you must decide how to defend. Your first task is to read the lie of the spade suit. If West's spades are headed by the king, you will want to win the first trick with the ♠J and to continue with ace and another spade. You will then score at least four spade tricks, giving the defence a very good start.

Suppose you take the trouble to apply the Rule of Eleven before embarking on this line of defence. If the ♠7 is indeed a fourth-best card, the North, East and South hands will contain four cards in spades that are higher than the seven. In your own hand and the dummy, you can already see five such cards. You can therefore conclude that the ♠7 is not a fourth-best card at all. It must instead be a second-best card from weakness. West will hold either ♠9–7–x or ♠9–7–x–x.

Since there is no prospect for the defence in the spade suit, you should rise with the ♠A at Trick 1. The only chance of scoring several tricks for the defence now lies in the heart suit and you therefore switch to the ♥Q. When the cards lie as in the diagram, this smart defence will be rewarded. You and your partner will score four

heart tricks, putting the 3NT contract one down. If instead you were to play the ♠J on the first trick, declarer would win with the ♠K and quickly add four more tricks in each minor suit to make the contract.

**Above:** East can see five cards higher than the ♠7. He therefore knows that the lead cannot be fourth-best from strength.

# CHOOSING BETWEEN ACTIVE AND PASSIVE DEFENCE

There are many positions where it will cost the defenders to make the first play in a suit. Suppose that, as declarer, you hold ♦J–8–3 in the dummy and ♦Q–6–5 in your hand. If you have to play the suit yourself, and the defenders hold one top honour each, you will probably make no trick at all from the suit. If instead the defenders make the first play in the suit, the defender in the third seat will have to rise with the ace or king. You will then be certain to score a trick with the queen or jack.

## When to defend passively

The defenders often have to make an important decision. Do they need to play actively, attacking a new suit to score tricks there? Or will they perhaps do better to play passively, leaving declarer to play the new suit himself? To answer this question, the defenders must try to determine whether declarer, left to his own devices, will be able to discard his potential losers in the key suit. Look at this deal:

**Right:** A passive defence. If West defends too actively here, attacking the diamond suit, he will give away the contract.

Sitting West, and defending the game in hearts, you lead the ♠Q, which declarer wins with the ♠K. He then leads a trump and you rise with the ♥A. The sort of defender who is always "trying another suit" might well switch to diamonds now. The effect is all too predictable. East would have to rise with the ♦A and declarer would then score a diamond trick, making the contract.

There is no need to play an active defence in this way because it is most unlikely that dummy's club suit can provide a discard of a diamond from the South hand. If declarer held three small diamonds and ♣A–Q doubleton, he would have taken a discard before playing trumps. Nor it is likely that he holds specifically ♣A–Q–J and can take a discard on the fourth round of clubs.

So, as West you do best to exit passively with a spade or a trump. Declarer will eventually have to play the diamond suit himself. He will lose three diamond tricks and go one down.

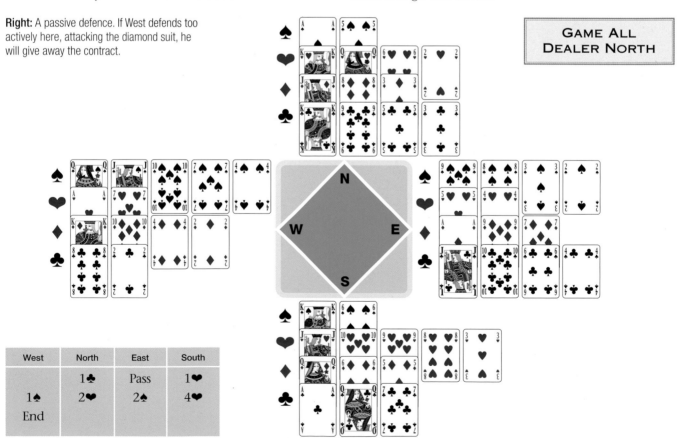

> **GAME ALL**
> **DEALER NORTH**

| West | North | East | South |
|------|-------|------|-------|
|      | 1♣    | Pass | 1♥    |
| 1♠   | 2♥    | 2♠   | 4♥    |
| End  |       |      |       |

## When to defend actively

To show the other side of the coin, here is a deal where the defenders do have to play actively. If they fail to do so, declarer will discard his potential losers.

West leads the ♦Q and, sitting East, you win with the ♦A. It is easy to predict what will happen if you exit passively with a trump or another diamond. Declarer will draw trumps and set up dummy's club suit, on which he can discard one or more heart losers.

You need to defend actively, attempting to set up some heart tricks before declarer can take discards on dummy's club suit. So, at Trick 2 you switch to the ♥4, South following with the ♥3. West plays the ♥10 and declarer is doomed to defeat, whether he wins the first or second round of hearts. When he eventually plays on clubs, you will win with the ♣A and cash a total of two hearts, one club and one diamond to beat the contract.

**Right:** An active defence. East must defend actively on this deal, attacking the heart suit to set up the defenders' winners in good time.

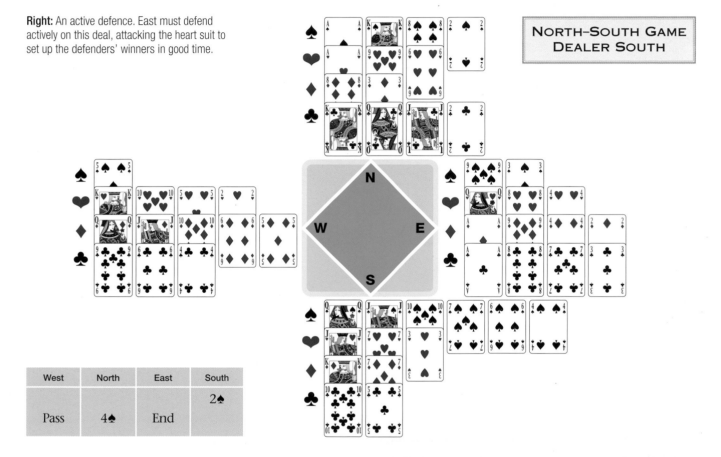

NORTH–SOUTH GAME
DEALER SOUTH

| West | North | East | South |
|------|-------|------|-------|
|      |       |      | 2♠    |
| Pass | 4♠    | End  |       |

### EXPERT IN TWO FIELDS
♠ ♥ ♦ ♣

No one has ever reached the very top level of both bridge and chess, although there have been many who played both games strongly. Guillaume le Breton Deschapelles excelled at whist and chess, however, in the early 19th century. He was rated the strongest player in France at both games, also at billiards despite losing his right hand during the Siege of Mainz.

**Right:** Germany's Daniela von Arnim. In partnership with Sabine Auken-Zenkel, she won the women's world championship in 1995 and 2001.

# WHEN TO COVER AN HONOUR WITH AN HONOUR

The advice sometimes given to beginners is "always cover an honour with an honour". In other words, if declarer plays an honour from one hand or the other the defender in second seat should cover with a higher honour. There are few hard-and-fast rules in bridge and, indeed, there are many exceptions to this one. Covering will often be a mistake.

### Cover to promote a trick

Let us see first how a cover can prove effective. Look at this club position:

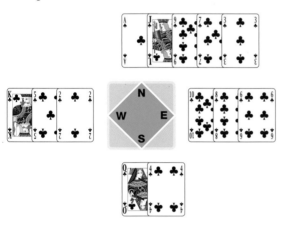

Declarer leads the ♣Q from his hand. If West fails to cover with the king, the queen will be run successfully. Declarer will finesse the ♣J on the next round and end with five club tricks. West should instead "cover an honour with an honour", playing his ♣K on the ♣Q. Dummy wins with the ♣A but East's ♣10 will now score a trick on the third round. The purpose of covering is clearly illustrated. You cover with the intention of promoting a lesser card, either in your own hand or in partner's.

The situation would be the same, of course, if the ♣Q and the ♣J were swapped. When South led the ♣J, West would cover in the hope of promoting the ♣10 with East. If South happened to hold ♣J–10 or ♣J–10–4, nothing would be lost. All five club tricks would be his, whatever the defence.

Suppose next that the ♣Q–4 were in the dummy, with declarer's club holding hidden from view. It would again be the correct defence to cover the ♣Q with the ♣K.

### Do not cover when no promotion is possible

When there is no such prospect of promoting a trick, you should not cover. Suppose declarer is playing in 4♠ or 6♠ with this trump suit:

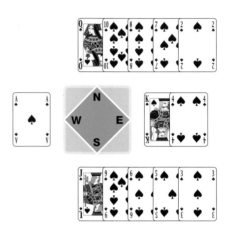

When the ♠Q is led from dummy East should not cover, because there is virtually no chance of promoting a trick by doing so. You can see what would happen if he did cover. West's ♠A would complete a heavily laden first round and declarer would lose only one trump trick. It is also possible that the spade suit lies like this:

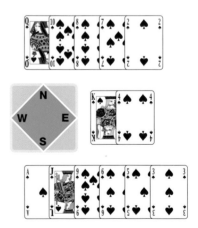

With only two cards missing, declarer has no intention of running the ♠Q. He has led it just in case you hold ♠K–4 in the East seat and are tempted to cover! Provided you follow smoothly with the ♠4, declarer will expect West to hold a singleton ♠K. He will rise with the ♠A and lose a trick in the suit when West shows out.

## Do not cover the first of touching honours

When declarer leads one of touching honours, it is usually wrong to cover:

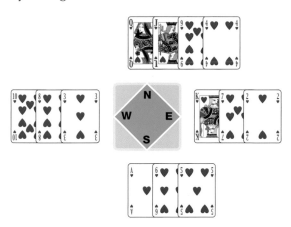

If East covers the ♥Q with the ♥K, declarer will win with the ace and subsequently finesse the ♥9 to score four heart tricks. East should not cover the first of touching honours. The queen is run successfully but declarer cannot then score more than three heart tricks. If he leads the ♥J on the second round, East will cover to promote his partner's ♥10.

It will also cost a trick to cover in this very common position:

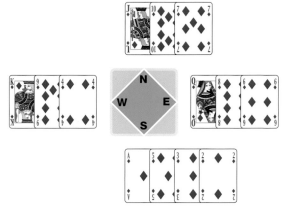

The ♦J is led from dummy. If East makes the mistake of covering with the ♦Q, declarer will win with the ace and lead back towards the ♦10. He will score three diamond tricks instead of the two that were his due. Again, East should not cover the first of touching honours. The ♦J is run to West's ♦K and declarer must now lose a second trick in the suit, however he continues.

---

### JAMES BOND'S SLAM ON 6 POINTS
♠ ♥ ♦ ♣

Perhaps the most famous bridge hand in literature is a version of the Duke of Cumberland's hand, which was used by card cheats for decades. In Ian Fleming's novel, *Moonraker*, James Bond rigs the deck to give villain, Hugo Drax, the East hand shown below:

```
              ♠ 10 9 8 7
              ♥ 6 5 4 3
              ♦ —
              ♣ 7 6 5 3 2
♠ 6 5 4 3 2           N        ♠ A K Q J
♥ 10 9 8 7 2      W     E      ♥ A K Q J
♦ J 10 9             S        ♦ A K
♣ —                           ♣ K J 9
              ♠ —
              ♥ —
              ♦ Q 8 7 6 5 4 3 2
              ♣ A Q 10 8 4
```

Bond, who holds the South hand, is pretending to be drunk. He bids a grand slam in clubs. Drax doubles, scornfully, and Bond redoubles. A large side bet is agreed in addition and the grand slam cannot be defeated! Declarer can establish the diamond suit and pick up East's ♣K–J–9 with two finesses.

**Above:** With 31 points in his hand, East cannot believe that 7♣ will be made against him.

# KEEPING THE RIGHT CARDS

One of the most important aspects of good defence is the ability to keep the right cards when you are forced to make some discards. One good guideline is that you should "match your length" with any length visible in the dummy. For example, if dummy contains ♠K–Q–8–2, you should not discard a spade from a holding such as ♠J–10–6–3. If declarer has the ♠A, your holding is necessary to guard the fourth round. Even if your partner holds the ♠A, you may still need all your spades to restrict declarer to the minimum number of tricks from the suit.

## Matching the dummy's length

Let us see an example of "matching dummy's length" in the context of the complete deal shown below.

You are sitting East and your partner leads the ♥Q. Declarer allows this card to win, hoping to tighten the end position and cause discarding problems for the defenders later. He wins the next round of hearts with the ♥K and cashes four rounds of clubs, followed by dummy's ♥A. You must now find a discard from ♠10–9–6–2 ♦Q–10–7.

**Right:** Matching the length in dummy. There are four spades in dummy and East should therefore retain all four spades.

Dummy has four-card spade length and you must retain your four spades, matching dummy's length, to avoid giving a trick away when declarer holds the king and queen of the suit. You may be surprised to hear that your ♦Q–10–7 are virtually worthless. If declarer holds the ♦A–K–J sitting over them, he can finesse in the suit anyway. Otherwise your partner will hold the ♦J and can guard the diamond suit himself. So, throw a diamond and retain your important spade guard. The slam will then go down.

---

### COUNT SIGNALS
♠ ♥ ♦ ♣

One of the important reasons for giving count signals (a high signal to show an even number of cards, a low signal to show an odd number) is to help your partner to decide which cards to retain. If your count signal implies that declarer holds three spades rather than four, for example, partner will not need to keep four spades.

---

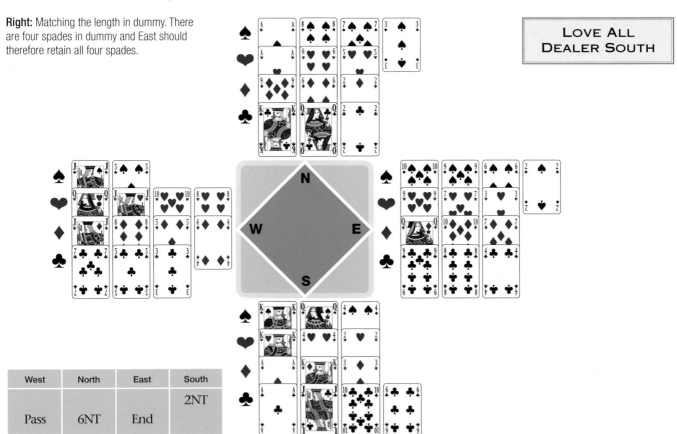

**LOVE ALL
DEALER SOUTH**

| West | North | East | South |
|------|-------|------|-------|
|      |       |      | 2NT   |
| Pass | 6NT   | End  |       |

## Making deductions from declarer's play

It is often possible to deduce declarer's length in a suit from the way that he has chosen to play the hand. Take the West cards on the deal shown below.

Sitting West, you lead the ♥Q against the spade slam. When this card wins the first trick, you play another heart, South ruffing. Declarer draws two rounds of trumps with the queen and jack. When you show out, throwing a diamond, he continues with three more rounds of trumps. You can safely throw all your hearts. On the last trump you must make one more discard from ♦Q–J–8 and ♣10–9–7–3. If declarer holds ♦A–K–10, you must keep your diamonds. If instead he holds ♣A–K–Q–x, you must keep your clubs. What would your decision be? If declarer did hold ♦A–K–10, he would have ruffed his diamond loser in dummy before drawing three rounds of trumps. So, you should throw a diamond and keep your potential guard in clubs. Declarer will then have no way to avoid a club loser and the slam will go down.

**Right:** Making a deduction from declarer's play. When declarer draws trumps without first taking a diamond ruff, West can deduce that South holds only two diamonds.

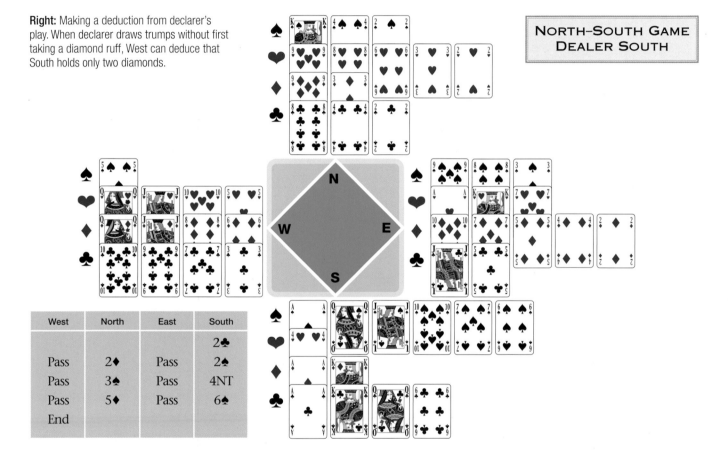

NORTH–SOUTH GAME
DEALER SOUTH

| West | North | East | South |
|------|-------|------|-------|
|      |       |      | 2♣    |
| Pass | 2♦    | Pass | 2♠    |
| Pass | 3♠    | Pass | 4NT   |
| Pass | 5♦    | Pass | 6♠    |
| End  |       |      |       |

---

### BRIDGE BOOK COLLECTORS
♠ ♥ ♦ ♣

Since the year 1900 about 8,000 books and pamphlets in the English language have been published on bridge. The most prolific decade was the 1930s, with around 1,400 publications. The world's three biggest bridge-book collections in private hands are owned by Tim Bourke of Canberra, Australia, by Wolf Klewe of Winchester, England and by Gerard Hilte, of Leerdam in the Netherlands.

**Right:** Tim Bourke of Canberra, Australian bridge expert and owner of one of the world's largest collections of bridge books.

# CHAPTER 4

# ADVANCED BIDDING

This section looks at some of the most popular bidding conventions from the tournament bridge world. First you will see the Cappelletti defence to 1NT, one of several conventions that allow you to contest the bidding after the opponents have opened 1NT. Next there is a discussion on how you can use bids in the opponents' suit to indicate strong hands in various situations. An important aid to bidding slams is Roman Key-card Blackwood, where you can ask not only about aces but also about the king and queen of trumps. Puppet Stayman allows you to detect a five-card major in the hand of the 2NT (two no-trumps) opener. Splinter bids tell your partner where you hold a shortage, thereby allowing him to judge if the two hands will fit together well. The chapter ends with a discussion of lead-directing doubles, where you double an artificial bid made by an opponent to tell your partner what opening lead you would like against the eventual contract.

**Right:** Employing the Cappelletti convention, the player has bid 2♣ to show a long suit somewhere. Partner's 2♦ asks the overcaller to specify which suit it is.

# CAPPELLETTI DEFENCE TO 1NT

The scoring table does not reward you very well when you defeat an opposing 1NT contract, particularly when the opponents are non-vulnerable. Whenever you take +50 or +100, defending 1NT, you will usually find that you could have scored at least +110 somewhere, playing the contract yourself. Apart from that, 1NT is a very difficult contract to defend. Declarer will often emerge with seven tricks when, with optimal defence, you could have set the contract. For these reasons, players are keen to contest the bidding when they hear an opposing 1NT bid. There are several conventions available and one of the most popular is the Cappelletti Defence.

### The Cappelletti Defence
Both in the second and the fourth seats, these are the possible actions when playing Cappelletti:

| | |
|---|---|
| Double | a penalty double |
| 2♣ | a single-suiter in an undisclosed suit (6–card suit) |
| 2♦ | both major suits (at least 5–4) |
| 2♥ | hearts and a minor suit (can be 4–5 or 5–4) |
| 2♠ | spades and a minor suit (can be 4–5 or 5–4) |
| 2NT | both minor suits (at least 5–5). |

### Partner shows a single-suiter
When partner bids 2♣, you can pass if you hold six clubs or more, bid 2♦ to ask him to indicate his long suit, or respond in a major with a long holding there. This is a typical sequence:

**Above:** The Cappelletti Defence was invented by Michael Cappelletti, who is an expert at both bridge and poker.

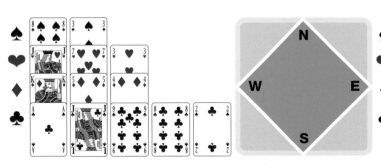

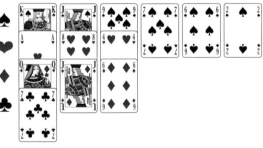

West's clubs are not long and strong enough to pass 2♣, particularly as he holds at least two-card support for whichever suit East may hold. As you can see, there is only a 5–1 fit in clubs, which will make nowhere near such a good trump suit as the 6–2 fit that exists in the spade suit.

To request partner's suit, West responds 2♦. East would pass this with long diamonds, but here he rebids 2♠ and this becomes the final contract.

| West | North | East | South |
|---|---|---|---|
| | 1NT | 2♣ | Pass |
| 2♦ | Pass | 2♠ | End |

## Partner shows both majors or both minors

When partner bids 2♦, showing both majors, you can pass with six diamonds and choose one of the major suits otherwise:

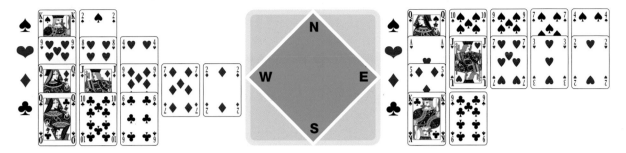

Sitting West, you give preference to hearts. This might sometimes be a 4–3 fit, yes, but that will not be your fault. You cannot always guarantee an 8-card fit somewhere.

| West | North | East | South |
|------|-------|------|-------|
|      | 1NT   | 2♦   | Pass  |
| 2♥   | End   |      |       |

Similarly, unless you hold a particularly strong hand, you will merely choose your better minor when partner overcalls 2NT.

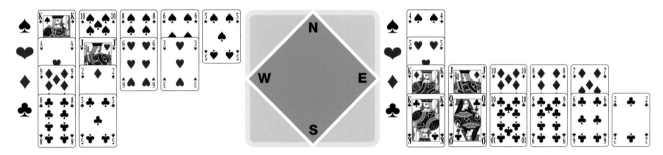

With two doubletons in the minors, there is some chance that you may be doubled. Bid 3♣ first, hoping that you escape a double. If you are doubled in 3♣, you will have to guess whether to try your luck in 3♦ instead.

| West | North | East | South |
|------|-------|------|-------|
|      | 1NT   | 2NT  | Pass  |
| 3♣   | End   |      |       |

## Partner bids 2♥ or 2♠

When your partner bids 2♥ or 2♠, showing a major–minor two-suiter, you will often pass. If you wish to discover his minor suit, you respond 2NT:

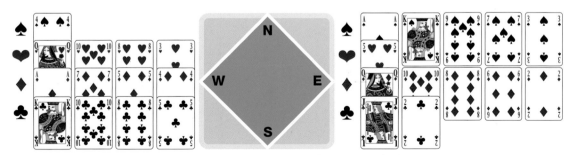

With a certain fit in one of the minors, West responds 2NT to ask East whether he holds diamonds or clubs as his second suit. East rebids 3♦, showing a two-suiter in spades and diamonds, and this bid ends the auction.

| West | North | East | South |
|------|-------|------|-------|
|      | 1NT   | 2♠   | Pass  |
| 2NT  | Pass  | 3♦   | End   |

# Cue-bid raises

Less experienced players hardly ever make a bid in a suit that has already been bid by the opponents. Since there are only five denominations available (the four suits and no-trumps), this is a big opportunity wasted. Serious bridge players hate to waste any possible call and make very good use of a cue-bid in the opponents' suit. Such a bid will nearly always show a strong hand. When your partner has already bid a suit, a cue-bid shows a strong raise of that suit.

**Above:** With a sound raise of partner's 1♠ overcall, East cue-bids in the opponents' suit.

### Cue-bid raise of an overcall

When partner has overcalled, as we saw earlier, any direct raise from you is pre-emptive. With a sound raise instead, you cue-bid the opener's suit. Let's see some typical sequences:

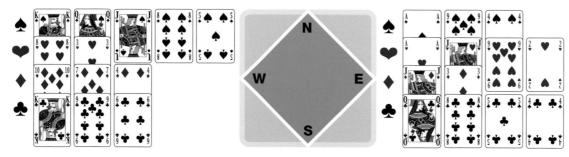

With 12 points and three-card spade support, East is interested in bidding a spade game. He shows his sound high-card raise with a cue-bid of 2♦. West has a minimum overcall and signs off in 2♠. East decides to bid no further, which is just as well because declarer could easily lose five tricks.

| West | North | East | South |
|------|-------|------|-------|
|      |       |      | 1♦    |
| 1♠   | Pass  | 2♦   | Pass  |
| 2♠   | End   |      |       |

When the overcall was made in a minor suit, the purpose of a cue-bid raise will normally be to investigate a possible 3NT contract:

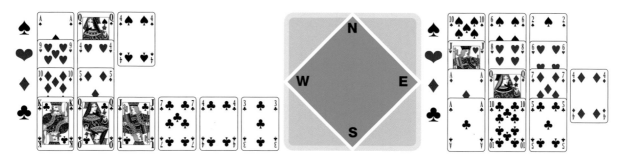

East makes a cue-bid in hearts, the opponents' suit, to show his sound raise in clubs. He hopes that West can rebid 2NT with a heart stopper. West has no reason to be ashamed of his overcall and shows his values in spades.

On some deals this would be enough for East to bid 3NT when he held a heart stopper himself. On this occasion neither player can stop the hearts and there is insufficient playing strength for a minor-suit game. Wisely, they stop in 3♣.

| West | North | East | South |
|------|-------|------|-------|
|      |       |      | 1♥    |
| 2♣   | Pass  | 2♥   | Pass  |
| 2♠   | Pass  | 3♣   | End   |

## Cue-bid raise of an opening bid

When your partner's one-bid has been overcalled, you have the opportunity to make use of a cue-bid response. Suppose the bidding has started like this:

| West | North | East | South |
|------|-------|------|-------|
| 1♠ | 2♦ | ? | |

A raise to 2♠ would show three-card support and around 5–9 points. A raise to 3♠ would be pre-emptive, showing 4-card support and around 4–8 points. With a stronger hand including spade support, you would cue-bid 3♦. Suppose you held one of these hands as East:

**1**

With hand (1) you would raise to 2♠.

**2**

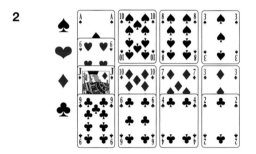

On (2) you would raise pre-emptively to 3♠, shutting out a possible heart fit for the opponents.

**3**

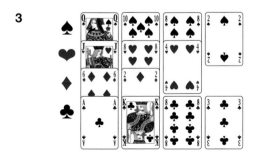

Hand (3) represents a genuine game-try hand in spades, with the values in high-card points. You would therefore cue-bid 3♦. Partner would then sign off in 3♠ when he held a minimum hand and would have passed the normal, uninterrupted sequence of 1♠ – 3♠.

A similar scheme is used when partner has opened 1♣ or 1♦. Suppose partner's 1♦ is overcalled with 1♥ and you hold one of these hands in the third seat:

**1**

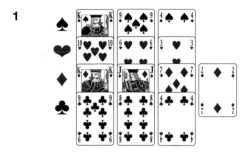

You would raise to 2♦ on (1).

**2**

With hand (2) you would raise pre-emptively to 3♦, which might well shut out an opposing spade contract.

**3**

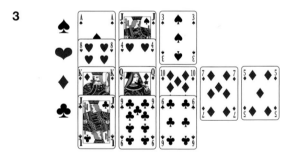

On (3) you cue-bid 2♥, showing a sound raise in diamonds with game ambitions.

---

### ROTH-STONE BIDDING
♠ ♥ ♦ ♣

The Unusual No-trump convention, where 2NT shows a two-suited hand in the lowest unbid suits, was invented by the American Alvin Roth in the 1940s. It was subsequently developed by his partner for many years, Tobias Stone. In the Roth-Stone bidding system, strong opening bids were advocated in the first and second positions. Roth and Stone would often pass 12-point hands.

# ROMAN KEY-CARD BLACKWOOD

In the original version of Blackwood, the responses stated only how many aces were held. When you are aiming for a slam in a suit, the king or queen of trumps can be just as important as an ace. A new version, known as Roman Key-card Blackwood, includes these two cards in the responses. It swept the tournament bridge world like wildfire and the time has come to take a look at it.

| 5♣ | 0 or 3 key cards |
|---|---|
| 5♦ | 1 or 4 key cards |
| 5♥ | 2 or 5 key cards and no queen of trumps |
| 5♠ | 2 or 5 key cards and the queen of trumps. |

## Asking for key cards

When a trump suit has been agreed, either player may bid 4NT (Roman Key-card Blackwood, hereafter shortened to RKCB) to ask how many key cards partner holds. There are five key cards: the four aces and the king of trumps. The table shows the responses.

There is rarely any ambiguity as to whether 0 or 3 key cards are held (or 1 or 4). If the 4NT bidder is uncertain, he may sign off in the expectation that partner will bid again when he holds the more generous allocation. Here is a typical RKCB sequence:

| West | East |
|---|---|
| 1♥ | 1♠ |
| 2♠ | 4NT |
| 5♠ | 6♠ |

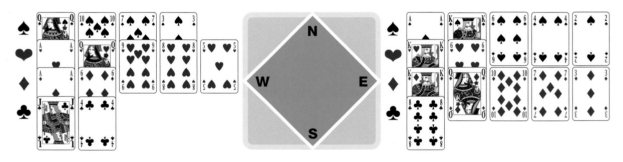

West's 5♠ response shows two key cards (two aces here) and the ♠Q. East is then prepared to bid a small slam.

Let's change West's hand, to give him a 5♣ response:

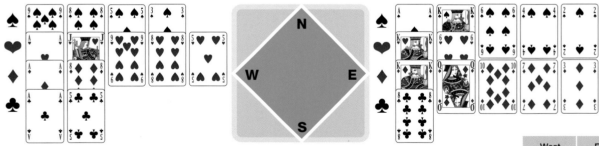

| West | East |
|---|---|
| 1♥ | 1♠ |
| 2♠ | 4NT |
| 5♣ | 5♠ |
| 6♠ | |

---

### EXCLUSION BLACKWOOD
♠ ♥ ♦ ♣

Exclusion Blackwood is a convention that allows you to ask for key cards even when you have a void in your hand. Instead of using 4NT as the enquiry bid, you jump to the five-level in the suit where you hold the void. In the auction 1♠ – 3♠ – 5♦, for example, the opener would be asking for key cards excluding the ♦A (a card of little value opposite a void).

---

When East hears the "0 or 3" response, it is possible if unlikely that West has no key cards. Playing safe, East signs off in 5♠. Since West holds three key cards rather than none, he advances to a slam anyway.

### Asking for side-suit kings with 5NT

When you bid 4NT and hear how many key cards partner holds, you can continue with 5NT to ask how many side-suit kings he has. You should do this only when all the key cards are present, otherwise there is no chance of a grand slam anyway.

> ### LEAP TO SEVEN
> ♠ ♥ ♦ ♣
>
> The 5NT bid, asking for side-suit kings, also confirms that all six key-cards are present. Responder is therefore entitled to jump to a grand slam when he has a source of tricks in his hand.

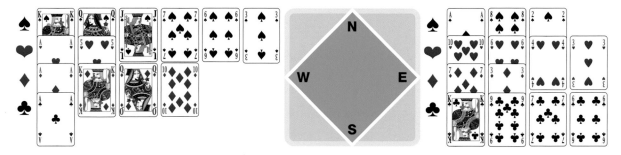

West bids 4NT and hears about the ace of trumps. He is willing to hope for the best in the diamond suit and therefore just needs to know whether a side-suit king is held. East admits to one king (5♣ = 0, 5♦ = 1, 5♥ = 2, 5♠ = 3) and the grand slam is bid.

| West | East |
|------|------|
| 2♣ | 2♦ |
| 2♠ | 3♠ |
| 4NT | 5♦ |
| 5NT | 6♦ |
| 7♠ | |

### Asking for the trump queen

When your partner's RKCB response is 5♣ or 5♦, he has not told you whether he holds the queen of trumps. You can continue with the cheapest bid not in the trump suit to ask whether the trump queen is held. Responder will sign off without the trump queen. With the queen, he will cue-bid a side-suit king or bid 5NT.

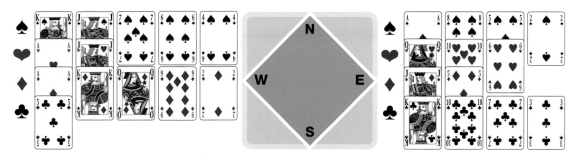

The 5♦ response tells West that an ace is missing. He is still willing to bid the slam, provided East holds the ♠Q. The sign-off in spades denies this card and West lets the bidding die at the five-level. Note that if East holds longer trumps than expected (five trumps rather than four in the present situation) he is entitled to pretend that he holds the trump queen. With ten spades between the two hands, there is a good chance that the defenders' ♠Q will fall on the first or second round. Even if a defender holds ♠Q–x–x, it may be possible to finesse the queen successfully.

| West | East |
|------|------|
| 1♠ | 3♠ |
| 4NT | 5♦ |
| 5♥ | 5♠ |

# TWO-SUITED OVERCALLS

Hands that contain two five-card suits are inappropriate for a take-out double, since partner is all too likely to respond in the short suit. It is therefore advisable to reserve certain bids to show specifically a two-suited hand. The most popular of these is the Unusual No-trump – a jump overcall of 2NT that shows the lowest two unbid suits. Almost as widely played is the Michaels cue-bid, which shows a two-suiter including any unbid major suit(s).

**Above:** With five cards in each minor suit, the player uses the Unusual No-trump convention.

### The Unusual No-trump
When an opponent has opened with one of a suit, a 2NT overcall in the second seat shows a two-suiter in the lowest two unbid suits. Although the point-count does not have to be as high as for an opening bid, the playing strength should be fairly sound because your partner will have to play at the three-level. Here is a typical example of the bid:

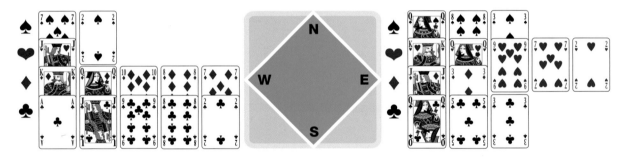

Although East has 10 points, he realizes that he is a long way from being able to suggest a game contract. He signs off at the three-level in his longer minor suit.

When the 2NT bidder has a very strong hand, he may indicate this by bidding again:

| West | North | East | South |
|------|-------|------|-------|
|      |       |      | 1♠ |
| 2NT | Pass | 3♣ | End |

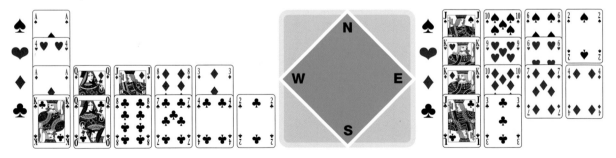

West raises to 4♦, announcing that he is very strong for a 2NT overcall. Although precision is not possible in such situations, East judges that his four-card trump support to the king entitles him to raise to game. This judgement proves sound and the game will probably be made unless the opponents score an immediate club ruff.

In the fourth seat (in an auction such as 1♠ – Pass – Pass – 2NT) the 2NT is normally played as natural, showing around 18–20 points.

| West | North | East | South |
|------|-------|------|-------|
|      |       |      | 1♥ |
| 2NT | Pass | 3♦ | Pass |
| 4♦ | Pass | 5♦ | End |

## Michaels cue-bids

When an opponent has opened 1♣ or 1♦, a Michaels cue-bid in the same suit (2♣ or 2♦, respectively) shows both major suits. Over an opening of 1♥ or 1♠ a cue-bid in the same suit shows a two-suiter containing the other major and one of the minor suits. Here are some typical sequences:

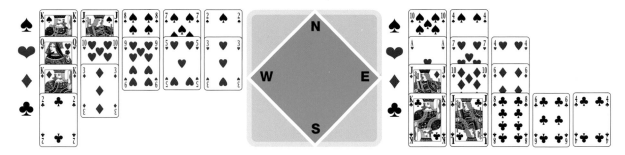

A Michaels cue-bid does not require as much playing strength as an Unusual No-trump bid, because the contract will usually be played one level lower, at the two-level. Here East responds at the minimum level in his better major. If West held 15 points or so, he might suggest a game by raising to 3♥.

| West | North | East | South |
|------|-------|------|-------|
|      |       |      | 1♦    |
| 2♦   | Pass  | 2♥   | End   |

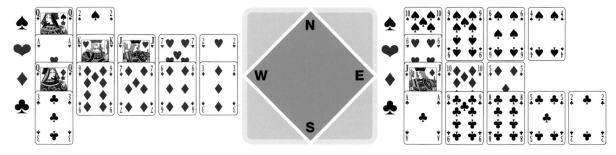

Opposite a major-suit Michael's bid, you may ask for a second suit by bidding 2NT. Here West shows diamonds and East is happy to pass out 3♦.

| West | North | East | South |
|------|-------|------|-------|
|      |       |      | 1♠    |
| 2♠   | Pass  | 2NT  | Pass  |
| 3♦   | End   |      |       |

### CONVENTION FORGOTTEN
♠ ♥ ♦ ♣

Even the top experts sometimes forget their conventions. At the 1957 European Championships, Terence Reese and Boris Schapiro were playing that a 4♥ response to 1NT was a transfer bid, showing spades. What is more, they had also agreed that anyone who forgot the method would have to pay a fine of 100 Austrian schillings. On one deal Schapiro did forget the convention, responding 4♥ on a hand with six hearts. When Reese rebid 4♠, Schapiro was nervous of bidding 5♥ in case this was taken as a slam try with spades agreed. Hoping to enlighten his partner, he bid 6♥. This was passed out and the contract was made when the Icelandic opponents failed to cash two aces. "Don't play the convention any more!" pleaded the rest of the British team. "No, no, we'll just increase the fine to 200 schillings," replied Reese.

### MICHAELS CUE-BID
♠ ♥ ♦ ♣

In most situations you show a strong hand when you cue-bid the opponents' suit. The Michaels cue-bid is an exception to this general rule and your hand may be quite modest.

# PUPPET STAYMAN

When you have a hand with 5–3–3–2 shape and 20–22 points, the only sensible opening bid is 2NT, even when the five-card suit is a major. In order to locate an eight-card fit when responder holds three cards in the suit, many tournament players use a modified form of Stayman opposite 2NT (and 2♣ – 2♦ – 2NT). It is known as Puppet Stayman and asks initially for a five-card major.

### Bidding 3♣ to ask for a five-card major

The rebids by the opener after a start of 2NT – 3♣ are:

| | |
|---|---|
| 3♦ | "I have at least one 4-card major but no 5-card major." |
| 3♥ | "I have five hearts." |
| 3♠ | "I have five spades." |
| 3NT | "I have no 4-card or 5-card major." |

Here are some typical sequences:

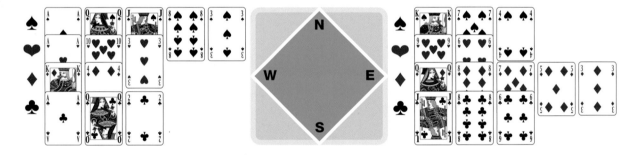

The 5–3 spade fit is discovered and 4♠ proves a better prospect than 3NT, which might fail on a heart lead. If West had bid 3♦ instead, showing at least one four-card major, East would have signed off in 3NT.

| West | East |
|---|---|
| 2NT | 3♣ |
| 3♠ | 4♠ |

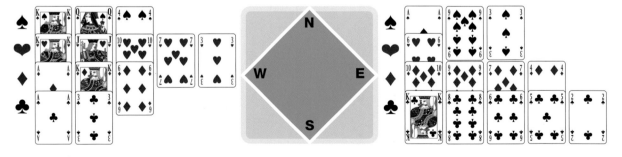

East would be happy to play in a 5–3 spade fit, in case the hearts are underprotected. When West shows five hearts, this fear vanishes and East bids the game in no-trumps. If West had rebid 3NT, denying even a four-card major, East would again play in 3NT since an 11-trick game in a minor suit is unattractive. Opposite a 3♦ rebid, East would have to seek a 4–3 spade fit or take his chances in 3NT.

| West | East |
|---|---|
| 2NT | 3♣ |
| 3♥ | 3NT |

## Locating a 4–4 fit

When the bidding has started 2NT – 3♣ – 3♦, there is still enough bidding space to locate any 4–4 fit that may be present. A slightly complicated mechanism is used to ensure that the 2NT opener becomes the declarer. These are the continuations by responder:

| 3♥ | "I have a four-card spade suit." |
|---|---|
| 3♠ | "I have a four-card heart suit." |
| 4♦ | "I have four hearts and four spades." |

As you see, the responder bids three of the major suit that he does not hold. It may seem strange but the "puppet mechanism", as it is called, works very well. Here are some typical sequences:

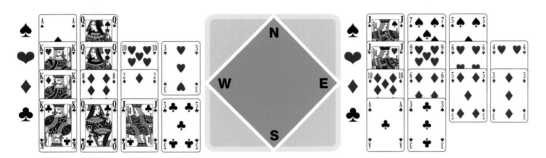

| West | East |
|---|---|
| 2NT | 3♣ |
| 3♦ | 3♠ |
| 4♥ | |

When West rebids 3♦, saying that he holds at least one four-card major, East bids 3♠ to indicate a four-card heart suit. West duly bids the heart game and his ♦K is protected from the opening lead.

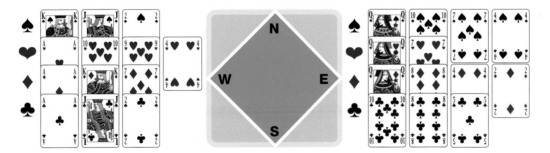

| West | East |
|---|---|
| 2NT | 3♣ |
| 3♦ | 3♥ |
| 3NT | |

East bids 3♥ to show a four-card spade suit. No 4–4 fit has come to light and West therefore bids 3NT, which ends the auction.

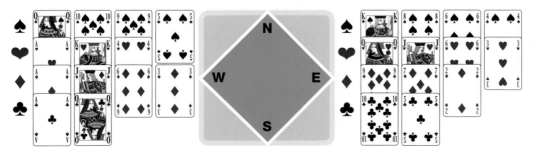

| West | East |
|---|---|
| 2NT | 3♣ |
| 3♦ | 4♦ |
| 4♠ | |

East shows both four-card majors and West bids game in spades. The strong hand will be hidden from view.

# SPLINTER BIDS

When two bridge hands fit well together, the trick-taking potential is greater than you might expect from the number of points held. One aspect of two hands fitting well is that little honour strength in one hand is wasted opposite a shortage. Suppose declarer holds ♦A–8–7–2 and the dummy holds ♦6. That represents an excellent fit. The ace will win the first round and the low cards can be ruffed. Suppose instead that declarer holds ♦K–Q–8–4 opposite a singleton. One point more in the suit, yes, but the fit is very poor. Not only will the first round now be lost, the king and queen may well be worth very little. They could have been ruffed anyway.

A "splinter bid" shows where you hold a side-suit singleton (or void). Your partner will then be able to assess whether the two hands fit well together. If they do, a slam may be possible. This is the scheme of splinter-bid responses after partner has opened bidding with 1♠:

| 4♣ | shows a sound game raise with at most one club |
|---|---|
| 4♦ | shows a sound game raise with at most one diamond |
| 4♥ | shows a sound game raise with at most one heart. |

A typical splinter bid by responder suggests around 10–14 points. Suppose partner has opened 1♠ and you hold one of these hands:

**1**

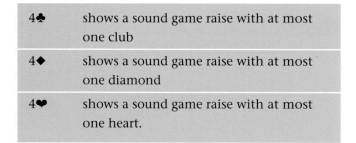

You would respond 4♣ on (1), showing a sound raise to game in spades and at most one club. Similarly, you would respond 4♦ on (2). The values in (3) are not quite sufficient for a game raise and you would respond just 3♠.

**Above:** A splinter bid of 4♣ will allow the opener to judge how well the two hands fit.

**2**

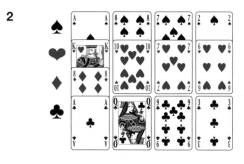

**3**

Over an opening bid of 1♥, the three splinter bids would be 3♠, 4♣ and 4♦. You may also agree to play splinter bids over an opening bid in a minor suit. Over 1♦, for example, the splinter bids would be 3♥, 3♠ and 4♣.

Let's see a couple of full auctions that involve a splinter bid by responder. In both cases the opener is able to judge whether the two hands fit together well.

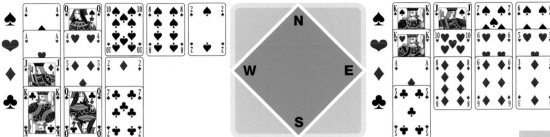

| West | East |
|------|------|
| 1♠ | 4♣ |
| 4♠ | |

West has a respectable opening bid but his ♣K–Q–7 represents a poor fit with partner's announced shortage in the suit. He therefore signs off in game.

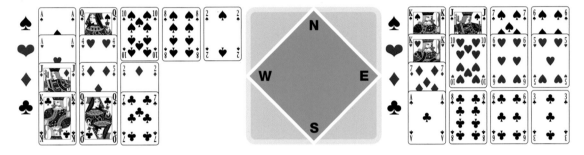

| West | East |
|------|------|
| 1♠ | 4♦ |
| 4NT | 5♥ |
| 6♠ | |

When East's minor suits are switched, West has only one point wasted opposite the shortage and knows that the hands will fit very well. He bids Roman Key-card Blackwood, hearing of two key cards (the ♠K and the ♣A). He then advances to 6♠, in the reasonable expectation that there will be only one trick to be lost – in diamonds. This does indeed prove to be the case and an excellent slam is made on a combined total of just 27 points.

## Splinter bid by the opener

The opener can make a splinter bid, when he has a good fit for responder's suit:

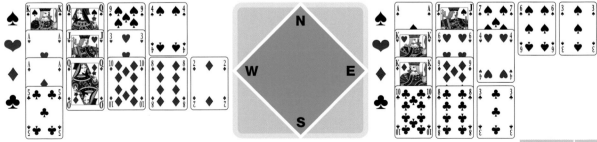

| West | East |
|------|------|
| 1♦ | 1♠ |
| 4♣ | 4NT |
| 5♣ | 6♠ |

A rebid of 3♣ by West would have been natural and game-forcing. The higher bid of 4♣ is therefore available as a splinter bid. It shows a sound raise to 4♠ and at most one club. With three low cards in the splinter suit, East diagnoses a fine fit and heads for a small slam.

# LEAD-DIRECTING DOUBLES

Even when you hold a poor hand, there are two good reasons to pay attention when the opponents are engaged on some lengthy auction. The first is that you may be able to use the information gained, when the time comes to defend their contract. Another reason is that you may have the chance to double a conventional bid, in order to suggest a good opening lead to your partner.

### Doubling a transfer bid or Stayman

When the opponents are playing a strong 1NT, it is normal to play a double of a transfer bid or of a Stayman 2♣ as lead-directing:

| West | North | East | South |
|------|-------|------|-------|
|  | 1NT | Pass | 2♣ |
| Dble |  |  |  |

West's double of the artificial 2♣ bid suggests a club opening lead. If South had responded 2♦ instead, a transfer bid to show long hearts, West would double when he held strong diamonds.

When North instead has opened with a weak 1NT, it is better to play that a double of Stayman or a transfer bid shows a hand that would have made a

penalty double of 1NT. In other words, a double shows upwards of 15 points and says nothing whatsoever about your holding in the suit artificially bid.

### Doubling a fourth-suit bid

When the opponents bid the fourth suit, you will have another chance to double. Do so when you hold strength in the suit and would like partner to lead it.

| West | North | East | South |
|------|-------|------|-------|
|  | 1♦ | Pass | 1♠ |
| Pass | 2♣ | Pass | 2♥ |
| Dble |  |  |  |

West has good hearts and doubles to suggest a lead of this suit.

### Doubling a strength-showing cue-bid

When your partner has overcalled, the next player will sometimes cue-bid in the same suit to show a sound raise. When you would like partner to lead the suit he has bid, because you hold an honour there, you can double the cue-bid.

| West | North | East | South |
|------|-------|------|-------|
|  | 1♠ | 2♣ | 3♣ |
| Dble |  |  |  |

---

**TAKE-OUT DOUBLES FORBIDDEN**

♠ ♥ ♦ ♣

In the early days of bridge, the staid and very conservative Portland Club (in London) decried the use of any conventional calls. Even the humble take-out double was not permitted in any bridge game that took place on their premises.

---

South shows a strong spade raise with his cue-bid in the suit that East has bid. Holding a doubleton ace in partner's suit, you would welcome a club lead. You announce this by doubling the cue-bid. Suppose instead that you had held two or three low cards in clubs. You would then have passed the cue-bid, letting partner know that you had no particular reason to welcome a club lead.

### Doubling a Blackwood response or control-showing cue-bid

When an opponent responds to Blackwood, and your partner may be on lead against the eventual slam, you will again have a chance to double.

| West | North | East | South |
|------|-------|------|-------|
|      | 1♠    | Pass | 3♠    |
| Pass | 4NT   | Pass | 5♦    |
| Dble |       |      |       |

You double the 5♦ response to suggest a diamond lead. Similarly, you can double a control-showing cue-bid.

| West | North | East | South |
|------|-------|------|-------|
|      | 1♥    | Pass | 4♥    |
| Pass | 4♠    | Pass | 5♣    |
| Dble |       |      |       |

Since South is likely to hold the ♣A, you are willing to double the control-showing cue-bid when holding just the king, sitting over the ace. Such a double is only worthwhile because your partner will be on lead against the eventual heart contract.

If you failed to double 5♣, on the above sequence, partner would be entitled to draw the negative inference that you had no particular liking for a club lead.

**Below:** Holding the ♣K over South's likely ♣A, you double to suggest a club lead to partner.

# Chapter 5

# Advanced card play

A skilled declarer looks everywhere for clues as to how he should play the hand. Here you will see how important clues can be drawn from the bidding. The next topics are how to create extra entries to the dummy, and how you can maintain control of the trump suit. You will see also how you can combine two different chances of making a contract, which is nearly always better than relying on just one chance. You will learn how to perform an elimination play, where you force a defender to make the first lead in a suit that you do not want to play yourself. Finally you will see the squeeze, the most famous card play technique in the game.

**Right:** The defenders have launched a forcing defence and declarer must be careful not to lose trump control.

# Clues from the bidding

When you are declarer, one of your tasks is to build a picture of the defenders' hands. The opening lead is usually quite informative. Every time a player shows out of a suit, you move closer to obtaining a complete count on the hand. Another important source of information comes from any bids that the defenders made. In particular, when a defender has shown length in one suit (perhaps with a pre-emptive opening, or an overcall), he is likely to be shorter than his partner in any other suit.

**Right:** Length in one suit implies shortage elsewhere. East's pre-emptive opening shows long clubs and he will be correspondingly short in the other three suits.

Look at the deal below, where East has made a pre-emptive opening of 3♣, suggesting a weak hand and seven cards in the club suit.

West leads the ♣8 and you win East's ♣10 with the ♣A. Since there are at least three losers in the side suits, the first task is to pick up the trump suit without loss. With nine cards between the hands, you would normally play to drop a missing queen. This is only a 52 per cent chance, compared with 48 per cent for finessing one or other defender for the card.

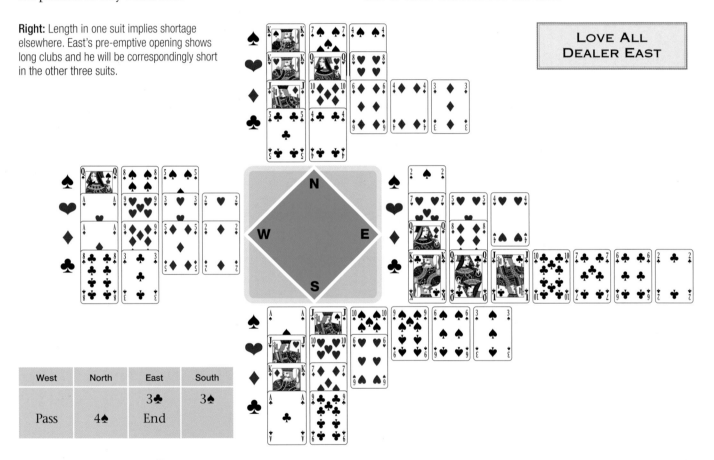

LOVE ALL
DEALER EAST

| West | North | East | South |
|------|-------|------|-------|
|      |       | 3♣   | 3♠    |
| Pass | 4♠    | End  |       |

---

### BEER CARD
♠ ♥ ♦ ♣

Among youth players, the seven of diamonds is known as the "beer card". When declarer makes his contract and scores the final trick with the seven of diamonds, his partner has to buy him a beer. Similarly, if a contract is defeated and a defender scores the last trick with the seven of diamonds, his partner too must buy him a beer. If the contract was doubled or redoubled, the drink order must reflect this.

---

Once a defender is known to be long in one of the side suits, the odds switch in favour of a finesse.

Here you expect East to hold seven clubs to West's two, so West is likely to hold longer spades than East. (You can see that, in fact, West is longer than East in all three of the suits outside clubs which predominates here.) You should therefore cash the ♠A and then run the ♠J.

This play proves successful and you draw West's last trump with dummy's ♠K. To make the contract, you now have to escape for just one diamond loser.

When the missing diamond honours are split between the two defenders, you will need to guess whether to run the ◆J or to lead towards the ◆K. Again the bidding will give you a big clue as to the lie of the diamond suit. If East held seven clubs to the K–Q–J and an ace, he would probably have rated his hand as too strong for a pre-emptive opening. It is therefore better to play him for the ◆Q. You run the ◆J and this does indeed force the ◆A from West. The contract is yours.

It can be just as important to bear in mind that a defender did not make a bid when he had the chance. On the deal shown below, for example, East did not find a response to his partner's opening bid. Since he would normally have done so when holding 6 points or more, it is reasonable for declarer to infer that he must hold fewer points than this.

**Right:** A deduction from the bidding. Declarer makes a valuable deduction from the fact that East did not respond to his partner's opening bid.

### REMEMBER THE BIDDING
♠ ♥ ♦ ♣

At every stage of playing a contract, make sure that your card-reading for the defenders' hands agrees with any bids that they have made. It should also be consistent with any bids that they have declined to make. For example, suppose that a defender has shown up with 10 points outside hearts and he did not open the bidding. He is unlikely to hold the ♥Q in addition. You should therefore finesse the other defender for the missing queen. The same sort of inference can be drawn when a defender declined to overcall or to make a take-out double.

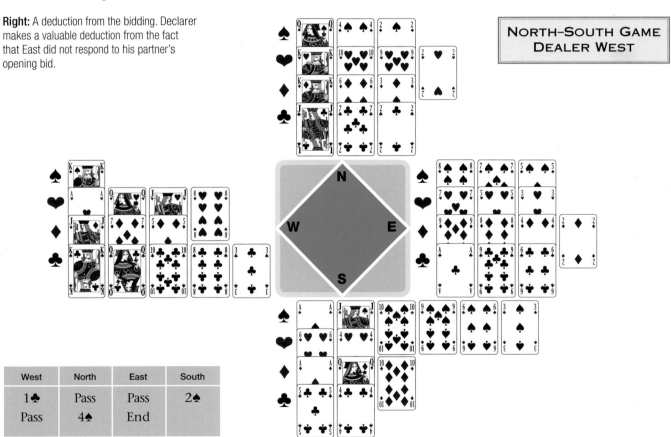

NORTH–SOUTH GAME
DEALER WEST

| West | North | East | South |
|------|-------|------|-------|
| 1♣ | Pass | Pass | 2♠ |
| Pass | 4♠ | End | |

An optimistic auction carries you to a game in spades and West leads the ♣K. East encourages with the ♣9 and West continues with the ♣Q and a third round of clubs to East's ace. You ruff in the South hand and see that you have three certain losers in the side suits. You will therefore need to pick up the trump suit without loss. Normally, with four cards missing, you would finesse East for the ♠K. Think back to the bidding, though. If East held an ace and a king in his hand, he would have responded to West's opening bid. West must therefore hold the ♠K and the only chance of making the contract is that the card is singleton. You play the ♠A from your hand and, as if by magic, the ♠K does indeed fall from the West hand. You draw trumps in two more rounds and concede a trick to West's ♥A, making the game exactly.

# CREATING EXTRA ENTRIES

When you are short of entries to the dummy (or to your hand), there are various techniques available to create an extra entry. Some of these involve conceding a trick in a suit that could otherwise have been cashed from the top. Here is an example:

**Right:** Sacrifice to gain an entry. By giving up a trump trick unnecessarily, declarer conjures an extra entry to dummy.

West leads the ◆J against your contract of 6♠ and you win with the ◆A. If you continue with the ace and king of trumps, there will be no way to avoid two subsequent heart losers. You will go one down. Instead you must seek a way to reach dummy's king and queen

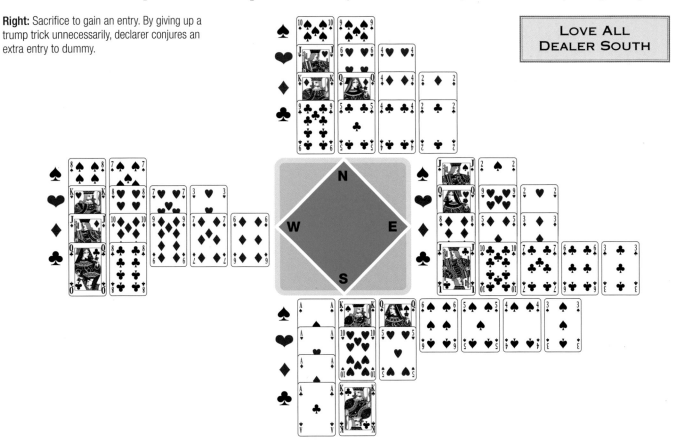

LOVE ALL
DEALER SOUTH

---

of diamonds. It is easily done in the trump suit. At Trick 2 you should lead a low trump from your hand. Dummy's ♠10 loses to the ♠J and East returns a heart. You rise with the ♥A, cross to the ♠9 and discard your two heart losers on the ◆K–Q. The slam is yours.

You would make the same play (a low trump from your hand) when dummy held only ♠10–2. You would then make the contract when West held the ♠J and dummy's ♠10 could therefore be set up as an entry. In both cases you would give away an unnecessary trick in the trump suit but gain two diamond tricks in return.

(It is interesting to note that a trump lead would have beaten the contract, provided East is alert enough not to play his ♠J on the first trick! Declarer is then given the entry to dummy while the diamond suit is still blocked.)

Right: Overtaking to gain an entry. By overtaking the honour cards in clubs, declarer can create extra entries to the dummy.

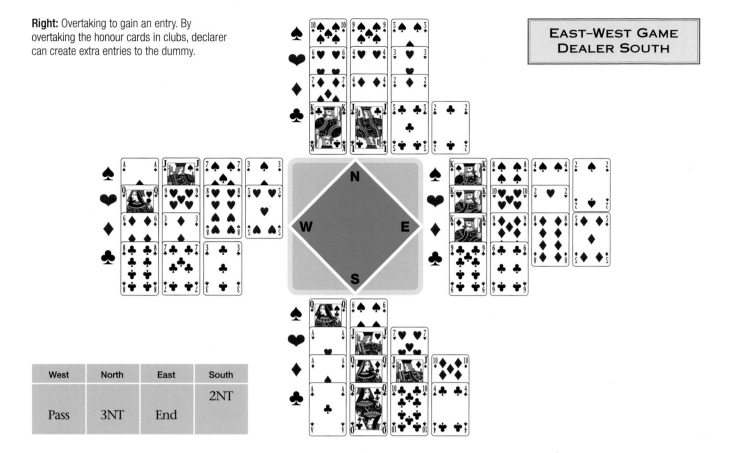

| West | North | East | South |
|------|-------|------|-------|
|      |       |      | 2NT   |
| Pass | 3NT   | End  |       |

Extra entries may also be conjured by overtaking honour cards. On the deal shown above, you can create three entries to dummy by playing the club suit in clever fashion.

West leads the ♠3 against your no-trump game and the defenders take four spade tricks. You discard two hearts from the South hand and one heart from the dummy. The defenders switch to a heart, dislodging your ace, and you must now try to make four diamond tricks in addition to the four club tricks.

You need East to hold the ♦K, obviously. When he holds four cards to the king, you will need to reach dummy three times in order to take three diamond finesses. You begin by cashing the ♣A, following with dummy's ♣2. On the next round of clubs, you lead the ♣Q, overtaking with dummy's ♣K.

Both defenders follow suit, you are pleased to see, and you play a diamond to the queen, receiving further good news when the finesse wins. You next lead the ♣10, overtaking with dummy's ♣J. A finesse of the ♦J wins and you can now reach dummy for the third time by overtaking your ♣4 with dummy's ♣5.

Note that this play was possible only because you disposed of your queen and ten of clubs under dummy's king and jack. You take a third diamond

finesse, playing low to the ♦10, and the contract is yours. Suppose you were to swap the North and South club holdings, moving the ♣A–Q–10–4 to the dummy. You would then be able to reach dummy no fewer than four times in the club suit (provided the defenders' cards broke 3–2). You could lead the ♣K to the ♣A on the first round, the ♣J to the ♣Q on the second round, the ♣5 to the ♣10 on the third round and finally the ♣2 to the ♣4!

### KEEP THE LOWEST TRUMP
### ♠ ♥ ♦ ♣

Your lowest trump is often an important card that is worth preserving. Suppose your trump holding is ♠6–3–2 in the dummy and ♠A–K–Q–J–10–4 in your hand. If the defenders force you to ruff early in the play, it will often be right to take the ruff with a high trump. By preserving the ♠4, you would give yourself a possible route to the dummy. When the defenders' trumps broke 2–2, you would be able to cross to dummy on the third round of trumps, leading the ♠4 and overtaking with the ♠6.

# KEEPING TRUMP CONTROL

When a defender holds four trumps, he will usually lead his strongest side suit. His aim is to force declarer to ruff, thereby eventually causing him to lose trump control. Declarer can sometimes repel this attack by using the short-trump holding, usually in dummy, to absorb the force. Here is an example of this technique:

**Right:** By using the short-trump holding in the dummy, declarer can avoid being forced in the long-trump holding.

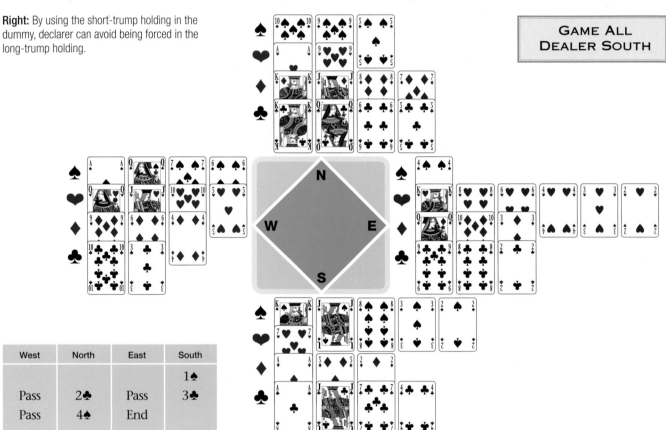

| GAME ALL |
| DEALER SOUTH |

| West | North | East | South |
|------|-------|------|-------|
|      |       |      | 1♠    |
| Pass | 2♣    | Pass | 3♣    |
| Pass | 4♠    | End  |       |

With a chunky four-card trump holding, West embarks on a forcing defence by leading the ♥Q. You win with dummy's ♥A and run the ♠10, West winning with the ♠Q. When West continues with a second round of hearts, you must play carefully. Suppose you ruff in your hand. When you play another trump, West will hold up the ace and East will show out. There will then be no way to make the contract. If you play a third round of trumps, West will win with the ace and force your last trump with another heart. You will then lose three trump tricks and a diamond, going one down.

To survive this hostile attack on your five-card trump holding, you must call for assistance from the dummy's trumps. When West leads a second round of hearts, you should throw a diamond from your hand instead of ruffing. A third round of hearts will cause no problem, because you can ruff in the dummy, thereby preserving your own trump length. It will then be a simple matter to knock out the ace of trumps and ruff the heart continuation in the South hand. You will draw West's last two trumps and claim the remaining tricks.

## THE LAST CHANCE
### ♠ ♥ ♦ ♣

When the famous player Oswald Jacoby reached the age of 80, he tended to make a bid each time it was his turn, whether he had the values or not. Tolerant as his partners were, they eventually asked him why he was bidding so much. "At my age the bidding may not get round to me again," he replied.

**Above:** Oswald Jacoby

On the next deal declarer's play in the trump suit is dictated by the need to use the short trumps in dummy to protect against a forcing defence.

**Right:** Declarer must give up a trump trick, while dummy's remaining trump will protect him against a continued force in hearts.

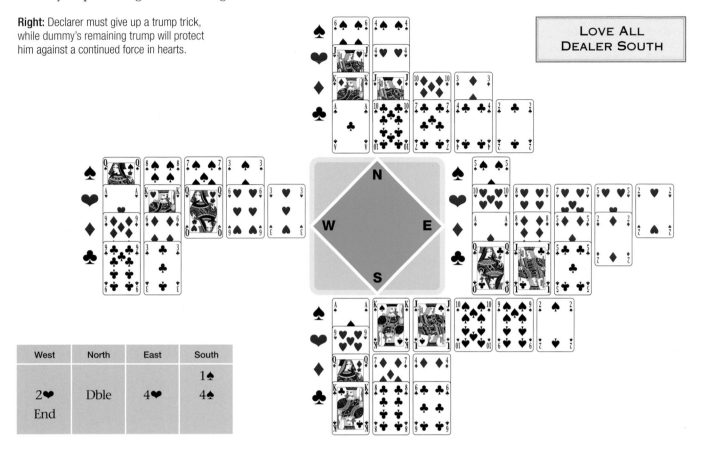

LOVE ALL
DEALER SOUTH

| West | North | East | South |
|------|-------|------|-------|
|      |       |      | 1♠    |
| 2♥   | Dble  | 4♥   | 4♠    |
| End  |       |      |       |

North makes a negative double on the first round, suggesting length in the minor suits. West leads the ♥A against the eventual spade game and continues with the ♥K (although a minor-suit switch would in fact work better). You ruff in the South hand and pause to consider your next move. If you play the ace of trumps, you will go down. When you continue with the king and jack of trumps, West will win with the ♠Q and force you with another heart. If you draw West's last trump then, you will have no protection against a heart continuation when you knock out the ◆A. If instead you play on diamonds without drawing the last trump, East will win and force your last trump with a heart, setting up a second trump for West.

To make the contract, you must lead the ♠J at Trick 3, giving up the trump trick that you can afford to lose at a moment that suits you. West wins with the ♠Q but cannot continue hearts effectively because you would be able to ruff in the dummy. When you regain the lead, you will be able to draw trumps and knock out the ◆A, making the contract easily.

**Above:** The defenders have launched a forcing defence and declarer must be careful not to lose trump control.

# ELIMINATION PLAY

One of the most important, and frequently occurring, card play techniques is that of elimination play. You begin by eliminating one or more of the side suits (either by removing them from your own hand and the dummy, or by removing them from the defenders' hands). You then throw a defender on lead. He cannot play an eliminated suit, either because he has no cards left in that suit or because it will give you a ruff-and-discard. He will therefore be forced to make the first play in another suit, thereby giving you a trick. Here is a straightforward example of elimination play:

**Right:** A typical elimination play. Declarer does not want to play the diamond suit himself and uses elimination play to force the defenders to play diamonds.

**Above:** The Aces team that won the 1971 Bermuda Bowl for the USA, defeating France in the final.

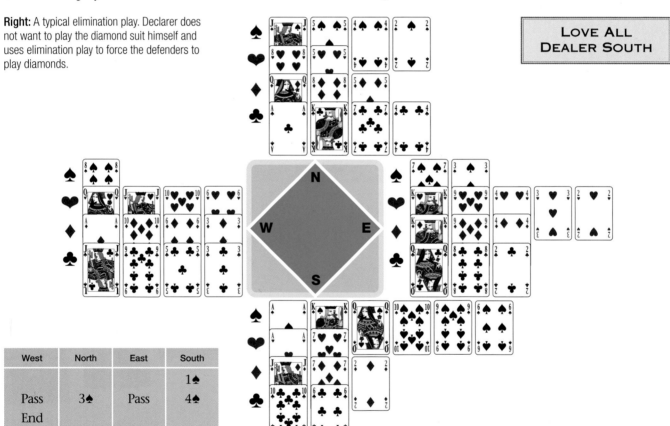

LOVE ALL
DEALER SOUTH

| West | North | East | South |
|------|-------|------|-------|
|      |       |      | 1♠    |
| Pass | 3♠    | Pass | 4♠    |
| End  |       |      |       |

West leads the ♥Q against your spade game. You have one loser in the heart suit and three more losers in diamonds, if you have to play the suit yourself. If the defenders had to make the first play in diamonds, however, you would be certain to score a diamond trick. By using elimination play, you can force them to do exactly that. Your plan will be to eliminate the black suits and then exit with a second round of hearts, forcing the defenders to win the trick.

---

**TRUMPS IN BOTH HANDS**
♠ ♥ ♦ ♣

An essential requirement for an elimination play end position is that you have at least one trump in both your own hand and the dummy. This means that the defenders cannot return an eliminated suit without giving a ruff-and-discard.

You win the heart lead and draw trumps with the ace and king. Your next task is to eliminate the club suit (so neither defender will be able to play a club when he is thrown in). You play the ace and king of clubs and ruff a club in your hand. You then cross to the ♠J and ruff dummy's last club. These cards remain to be played:

**Right:** Elimination ending. Declarer exits in hearts, forcing a defender to play a diamond (or give a ruff-and-discard).

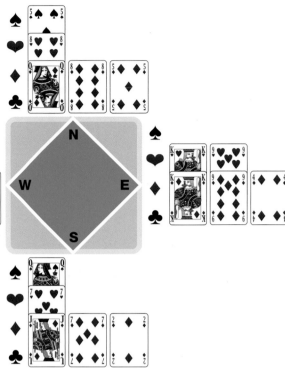

The preparation is complete and you now lead the ♥7. It makes no difference which defender wins the trick. A third round of hearts would give you a ruff-and-discard, allowing you to ruff in one hand and discard a diamond loser from the other. The defender who wins the trick will therefore have to play a diamond. You are certain to make a trick with the queen or jack and the game is yours.

Sometimes you can use elimination play to save you from having to guess in a suit. That is the situation here, where you have an apparent guess to make in the heart suit:

| West | North | East | South |
|------|-------|------|-------|
|      |       |      | 1♠    |
| Pass | 2♠    | Pass | 4♠    |
| End  |       |      |       |

**GAME ALL
DEALER SOUTH**

**Right:** Elimination play to avoid a guess. Declarer uses elimination play to avoid having to guess which defender holds the ♥Q.

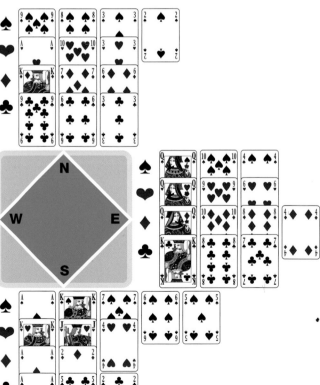

Sitting South, you win the ♣Q lead with the ace. When you play two rounds of trumps, you find that East has a trump trick. There are now three certain black-suit losers, so you will need to avoid a further loser in hearts. You could finesse either defender for the missing ♥Q. If you happened to guess wrongly, you would go down.

With the help of elimination play, you can avoid the need to guess in the heart suit. You play the ace and king of diamonds and ruff a diamond. Since diamonds are now eliminated from both your own hand and the dummy, neither defender will be able to play that suit without conceding a ruff-and-discard. These cards remain:

**Right:** Declarer exits in clubs, forcing a defender to play a heart (or give a ruff-and-discard).

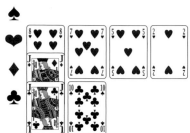

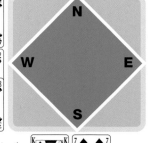

You exit with a club. The defenders are welcome to cash two club tricks and the trump queen. Since you still have a trump left in each hand, the defender left on lead will have to play a heart (or concede a ruff-and-discard by leading a diamond). You will then be assured of three heart tricks and the contract.

Look back at the two deals we have seen. On the first deal, diamonds was your "problem suit" – the suit that you very much wanted the defenders to play for you. On the second deal, hearts was the problem suit. Sometimes you throw a defender on lead with the first round of the problem suit itself. Look at this deal:

**EAST–WEST GAME
DEALER SOUTH**

**Right:** Exiting in the problem suit itself. Declarer hopes to avoid a loser in clubs and performs the elimination play by exiting on the first round of clubs.

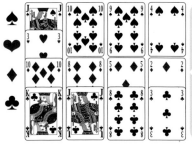

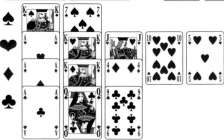

| West | North | East | South |
|------|-------|------|-------|
|      |       |      | 2♣    |
| Pass | 2♦    | Pass | 2♥    |
| Pass | 3♥    | Pass | 4♥    |
| Pass | 6♥    | End  |       |

You win the ♠J lead in your hand and note that there are two potential losers in the club suit. If you had to play clubs yourself, you would first finesse the ♣9, forcing the king when East held both the jack and ten of the suit. If a finesse of the ♣9 lost to the jack or ten, you would win West's return in a different suit and then finesse the ♣Q. As you see, such a line of play would not succeed here. You would lose two club tricks and go down. To make the contract, you should eliminate spades and diamonds before playing a club to the nine. If West wins with the ten or jack, he will not be able to return a spade or a diamond without conceding a ruff-and-discard. He will be forced to play a club instead.

You draw trumps in three rounds, which still leaves you with at least one trump in both hands (an important requirement of elimination play, so that you could benefit from a ruff-and-discard). You then cash the king and ace of spades and ruff a spade, eliminating that suit from the battlefield. When you continue with three rounds of diamonds, ending in the dummy, the spades and diamonds have been eliminated. The lead is in dummy and these cards remain:

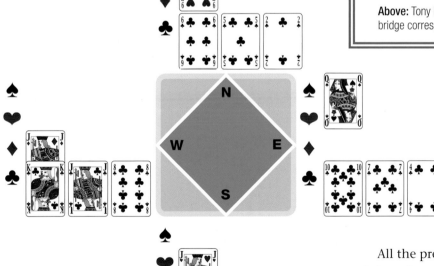

**Left:** By playing a club to the nine, declarer endplays West. He will have to return a club into the ace–queen tenace or give a ruff-and-discard.

All the preparation work is complete and you lead a club to the nine. West wins with the jack and has no safe return. A club will be into your ace-queen tenace and a diamond will give you a ruff-and-discard. It would do East no good to rise with the ♣10 on the first round of the suit. You would cover with the ♣Q and West would then have to lead into your ♣A–9 tenace when he won the trick.

# COMBINING DIFFERENT CHANCES

It is almost always better to combine two chances of making the contract, rather than relying on just one. This may involve taking the second-best chance in one suit because this will allow you to retain the lead and take advantage of your chance in another suit. That is what happens on this deal:

**Right:** Declarer combines two chances. Declarer takes the second-best chance in the trump suit, so that he can combine the additional chance of discarding the diamond loser.

West leads the ♦K against your game in spades. You win with the ace and see four potential losers, one in trumps and three more in the red suits. Looking at the trump suit in isolation, the best chance of avoiding a loser is to cash the ♠K and then to finesse the ♠J. If you follow this line and the finesse loses,

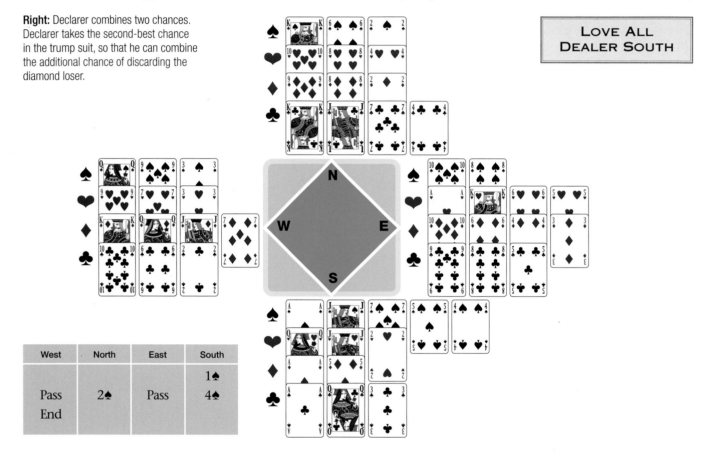

LOVE ALL
DEALER SOUTH

| West | North | East | South |
|------|-------|------|-------|
|      |       |      | 1♠ |
| Pass | 2♠ | Pass | 4♠ |
| End  |       |      |       |

## LUCK FACTOR REDUCED
♠ ♥ ♦ ♣

It was realized as long ago as 1857, in the days of whist, that the luck factor in card games could be reduced by playing each hand more than once and comparing results. Nowadays, nearly all competitive bridge (both for pairs and teams-of-four) employs this principle and is known as "duplicate bridge".

**Right:** Duplicate bridge. When the deal is over the cards will be returned to the board, ready to be played again at another table.

however, you will go down. When West wins with the ♠Q, the defenders will take one diamond trick and two hearts, beating the game.

A better idea is to begin with the second-best chance in trumps, playing the king and ace. If the ♠Q falls on the second round, which is quite a substantial chance, you will draw the last trump and make an overtrick. If the ♠Q does not fall, you will still be on lead. You will be able to take your second chance – discarding the diamond loser on the fourth round of clubs. With the cards lying as in the diagram you will be successful. West has to follow to three rounds of clubs and you throw the ♦5 on the fourth round of clubs, not caring whether West ruffs or not. You will lose just one trump and two hearts. By following the recommended line you make the contract when the ♠Q falls doubleton or when you can discard your diamond loser. That is a much better combined chance than relying solely on picking up the trump suit with a finesse.

It is sometimes important to combine your two chances in the right order. This is often the case when one chance will require you to lose an early trick in a suit. Look at the 6NT deal shown below, where you have prospects of an extra trick in both spades and hearts. You must seek to combine those chances.

West leads a safe ♦10 against 6NT. There are 11 tricks on top and two apparent chances of scoring a 12th trick. If East holds the ♠K, a finesse of the ♠Q will give you the slam. Another chance is that West holds the ♥Q. In that case a lead towards dummy's ♥J will yield the extra trick.

There is no need to choose between these chances. Provided you tackle the suits in the correct order, you can make the slam when either chance pays off. Suppose you win the diamond lead and finesse the ♠Q immediately. The finesse will lose and it will be too late to tackle the heart suit.

Since you will have to surrender a trick in hearts, even if the ♥Q is favourably placed, you should play that suit first. You win the diamond lead with the queen and lead a low heart towards dummy. Whether or not West chooses to rise with the ♥Q, you will score a third trick in hearts and make the slam. Suppose the cards had lain differently and the ♥J had lost to the ♥Q with East. You would still have been able to take your second chance in spades. That is because you would not need to lose the lead in order to take advantage of the ♠K lying with East. A finesse of the ♠Q would win and you could then cash the ♠A, scoring two tricks from the suit.

**Right:** Taking finesses in the right order. Declarer combines the chances in hearts and spades by taking the two finesses in the right order.

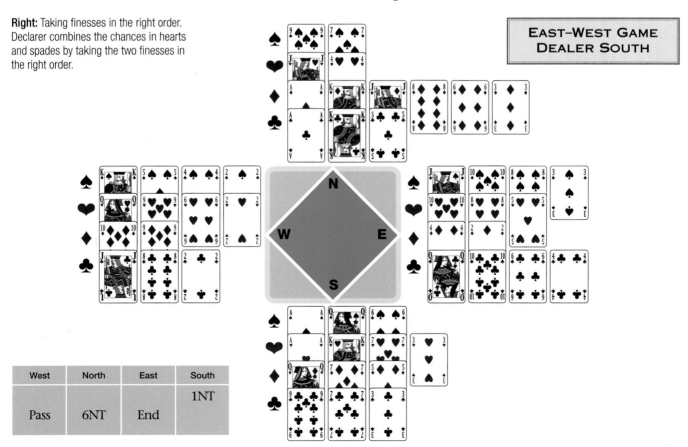

| West | North | East | South |
|---|---|---|---|
|  |  |  | 1NT |
| Pass | 6NT | End |  |

# THE THROW-IN

In an earlier section we looked at elimination play, where you threw a defender on lead at a time when both declarer's hand and the dummy still contained at least one trump. Because the defender could not afford to give a ruff-and-discard, he had to lead your problem suit, giving you a trick there. When one of the hands does not contain a trump, or the contract is being played in no-trumps, it is still possible to gain a trick by throwing a defender on lead. The play is then known, simply, as a throw-in. Here is an example:

**NORTH–SOUTH GAME DEALER EAST**

**Right:** A typical throw-in play. Declarer makes 3NT by throwing East on lead in clubs when he has no safe return to make.

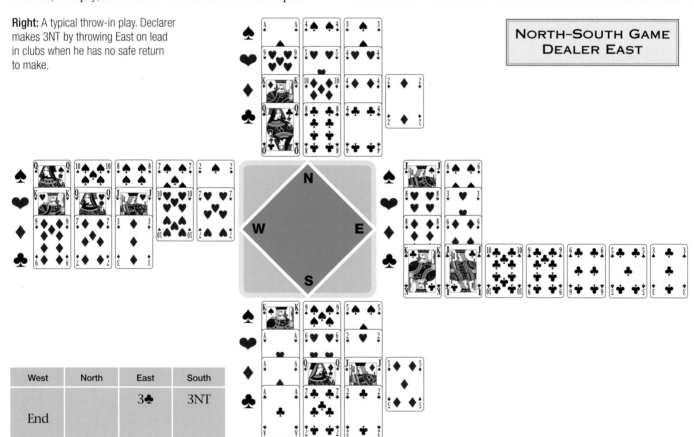

| West | North | East | South |
|------|-------|------|-------|
|      |       | 3♣   | 3NT   |
| End  |       |      |       |

West leads the ♥K. You duck the first two rounds of hearts and win the third round, East throwing a club. You have eight top tricks and the only serious chance of a ninth trick is to throw East on lead with a club, forcing him to lead away from the ♣K.

To prepare for a throw-in, you must remove East's possible exit cards in the other suits. You must hope that East has no more than two cards in spades. You begin with four rounds of diamonds and continue with the ace and king of spades. When East follows twice in each suit, as he did in hearts, it is a near

certainty that his shape is 2–2–2–7. In that case he will have nothing but clubs left in his hand. You lead the ♣2 from your hand and West does indeed show out. You play the ♣4 from dummy and East wins the trick cheaply. Since all his remaining cards are clubs, he must lead a club from the king. You run this to dummy's ♣Q and nine tricks are yours.

On the next example too, an opening bid by East allows you to be fairly certain of the lie of the cards.

West leads the ♥7 against your no-trump game. East plays the ♥10 and you allow this to win.

**Right:** Reading the cards after an opening bid. Declarer is able to diagnose a throw-in play on East because of the values shown by his opening bid.

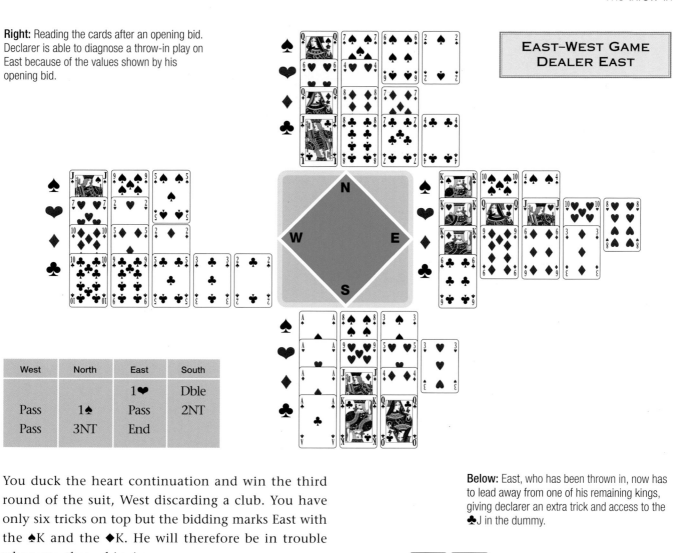

| West | North | East | South |
|------|-------|------|-------|
|      |       | 1♥   | Dble  |
| Pass | 1♠    | Pass | 2NT   |
| Pass | 3NT   | End  |       |

You duck the heart continuation and win the third round of the suit, West discarding a club. You have only six tricks on top but the bidding marks East with the ♠K and the ♦K. He will therefore be in trouble when you throw him in.

You cash the ♣A–K–Q and throw East on lead with a heart. He cashes his last heart winner and you discard a spade from your hand. Meanwhile, you have thrown two spades and a diamond from the dummy. These cards remain:

**Below:** East, who has been thrown in, now has to lead away from one of his remaining kings, giving declarer an extra trick and access to the ♣J in the dummy.

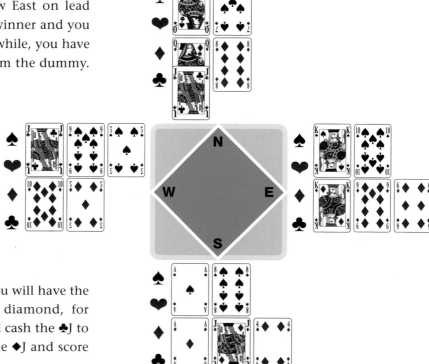

Whichever card East plays next, you will have the remaining tricks. If he plays a low diamond, for example, you will win with the ♦Q and cash the ♣J to throw a spade. You can then finesse the ♦J and score the ♦A at Trick 13.

# THE SIMPLE SQUEEZE

Perhaps the most famous play in bridge is the "squeeze". A defender who holds a guard on two of declarer's suits is forced to make a critical discard and has to release one of his guards. Here is a straightforward example:

NORTH-SOUTH
GAME
DEALER SOUTH

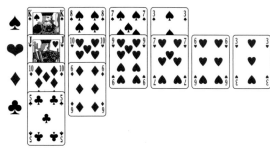

| West | North | East | South |
|------|-------|------|-------|
|      |       |      | 1NT   |
| Pass | 6NT   | End  |       |

**Above:** A typical simple squeeze. East holds the guards in clubs and diamonds and will have to throw one of them away.

You win the heart lead with the queen, cross to the ♣A and run the ♠Q, losing to the king. You win the heart return and see that you have 11 tricks on top, 12 if the clubs break 3–2 or the diamonds break 3–3. Before testing your luck in the minor suits, you should cash your spade winners. This position will result:

**Right:** Squeeze ending. When the ♠10 is led, East has to throw away one of his guards.

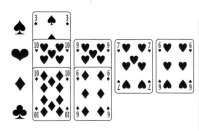

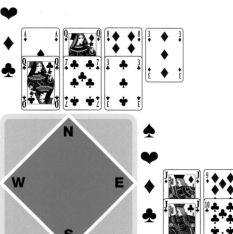

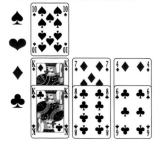

You cash the ♠10, throwing a club from dummy, and East is squeezed. He will have to throw a diamond or a club, releasing his guard in one of the suits. You will score your 12th trick from whichever suit he throws, making the slam.

An essential part of most squeezes is that you should lose at an early stage the tricks you can afford to lose. In other words, you should lose one trick in a small slam, four tricks in a 3NT contract. If you fail to do this, the defender with the two guards will have a spare card in his hand. He will not be squeezed when you play your last winner in the other suits. Look at this deal.

West leads the ♠10 against 6NT, East playing the ♠Q. Let's suppose first that you win immediately with the ♠A. You will not make the contract. West holds the guards in both the red suits but he will not be squeezed. When you play four rounds of clubs, West will discard his three remaining cards in spades. You will score only 11 tricks.

Before playing to Trick 1, you should make a plan. You have 11 top tricks and can make a 12th when the diamond suit breaks 3–3, or when the same defender holds at least four diamonds and four hearts. In the latter case you will be able to squeeze the defender, but only if you lose one trick early in the play.

**Right:** Rectifying the count. Declarer gives up a trick at an early stage, so West will have no spare card to throw later in the play.

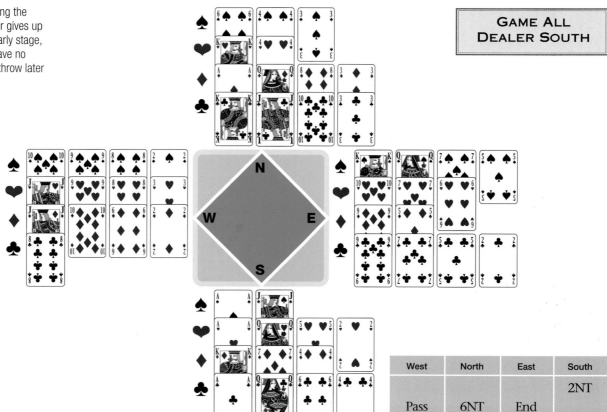

GAME ALL
DEALER SOUTH

| West | North | East | South |
|------|-------|------|-------|
|      |       |      | 2NT   |
| Pass | 6NT   | End  |       |

### BILL GATES
♠ ♥ ♦ ♣

Founder of Microsoft, Bill Gates, says: "Bridge is a game you can play at any age. If you take it up young, you will have fun playing it for the rest of your life. A lot of games don't have that depth. This one does." Gates competed in the 2002 world bridge championships in Toronto. In 2006 he partnered former world champion, Sharon Osberg, in the Verona world bridge championships. He told the press that programmers at Microsoft are working on sophisticated computer programs to play bridge.

**Left:** One of the world's richest men, Bill Gates is now a keen bridge player.

Now to see what happens if you duck the very first trick, allowing East to win with the ♠Q. You win the spade return and cash four rounds of clubs. The tableau to the right shows the position, where one club winner is still to be cashed. Because you ducked a round of spades at Trick 1, West has no card to spare when you lead the ♣Q:

**Right:** Squeeze ending. When the ♣Q is led, West has to abandon one of his red-suit guards.

West will have to throw one of his red-suit guards and you will then score your 12th trick from the suit he has abandoned. The action of deliberately losing one or more tricks, to tighten the eventual end position, is known as "rectifying the count".

If we strip that end position down to the basics, we can visualize the elements of a simple squeeze. Let's suppose that you cash the king, ace and queen of hearts and the diamond ace and king, before playing the ♣Q. The minimal end position shown below would result:

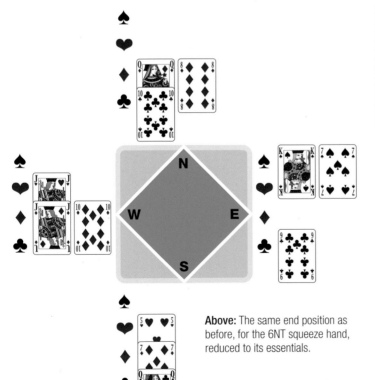

**Above:** The same end position as before, for the 6NT squeeze hand, reduced to its essentials.

Everything is now clearer. You have the three main elements of a simple squeeze:

- the "squeeze card" (♣Q), the card that you play to force a critical discard
- a "one-card threat" (♥5), guarded by West's ♥J
- a "threat with an entry" (♦Q–8) that lies opposite the squeeze card.

As before, West has no card to spare on the squeeze card (the ♣Q). If he throws a heart, the ♥5 in the South hand will become good. If instead West throws a diamond, you will score the last two tricks with dummy's ♦Q and ♦8.

---

### CHARLES SCHULTZ
♠ ♥ ♦ ♣

The cartoonist Charles Schultz was a keen bridge player and featured bridge in several of his Peanuts cartoons. His Snoopy character is the only "honorary lifemaster" of the American Contract Bridge League.

---

So, every time you plan a simple squeeze, you must look for a squeeze card, a one-card threat and a threat with an entry. It is all rather daunting on first acquaintance but after a while you will find it becomes easier. Opportunities for simple squeezes are very frequent and will give you many a tricky contract. Let's see one more example:

**Right:** The Vienna Coup. Declarer prepares for a heart–club squeeze by playing the ♥A, thereby freeing the ♥Q to act as a threat card against either defender.

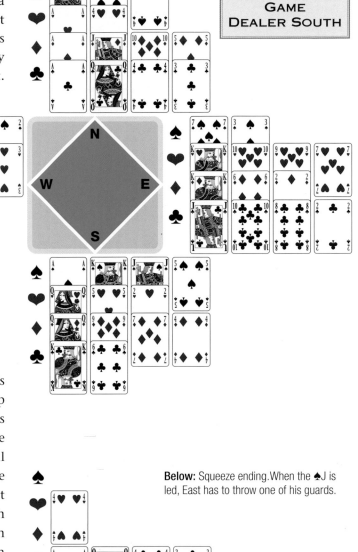

NORTH–SOUTH
GAME
DEALER SOUTH

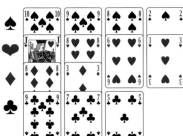

| West | North | East | South |
|------|-------|------|-------|
|      |       |      | 1NT   |
| Pass | 6NT   | End  |       |

You win the spade lead and run the ♦Q to East's ♦K, winning the diamond return. You have 11 top tricks and can score a 12th if the same defender holds the ♥K and the club guard. Try to visualize the components of the squeeze. The one-card threat will be the ♥Q. The "threat with an entry" will be dummy's club suit. The squeeze card will be the last spade. After playing dummy's top diamonds, you cash the ♥A to free your ♥Q as a one-card threat. You then play the remaining spades, arriving at the position shown in this tableau:

**Below:** Squeeze ending. When the ♠J is led, East has to throw one of his guards.

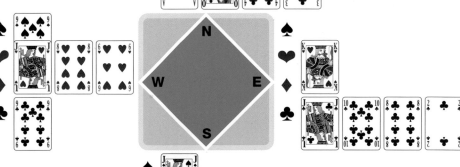

You play the squeeze card (the ♠J), throwing the ♥4 from dummy. East is squeezed and must discard one of his guards. If he throws a club, you will make four club tricks with the king, ace, queen and four of the suit. If instead he throws the ♥K, you will score a trick with the ♥Q.

# CHAPTER 6

# ADVANCED DEFENCE

Much good play at bridge involves counting. This is particularly true in defence, where you can count declarer's points to allow you to calculate which cards your fellow defender may hold. You will see why it is important to hold up high cards in defence and how to conduct a forcing defence, where you attack declarer's trump holding. When you hold a doubleton honour in defence, it is often right to throw the high card away, rather than risk being end-played with it later. Another important topic is how you can break declarer's communications, in particular by attacking an entry to dummy. Finally the two main ways in which the defenders can promote extra trump tricks for themselves are discussed – the straightforward trump promotion, where a defender is threatening to overruff, and the more spectacular "uppercut".

**Right:** East unblocks the ♠K on his partner's ♠Q lead. If he fails to do so, he will win the second round and be unable to continue the suit.

# COUNTING DECLARER'S POINTS

Counting is an important part of the game, for the defenders as well as for declarer. By counting declarer's points and comparing this total with the points indicated in the bidding, the defenders can often tell which line of defence has the best chance.

## Ruling out a defence by counting points

Take the East cards on this deal and see how you fare.

**Right:** Counting points to determine the right defence. East diagnoses the winning defence by counting declarer's points and ruling out a continuation of partner's suit.

GAME ALL
DEALER SOUTH

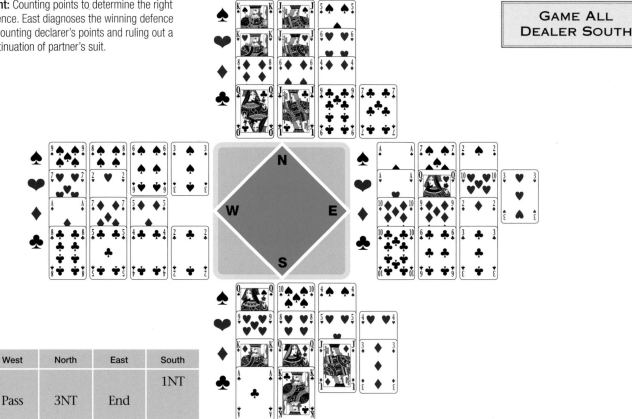

| West | North | East | South |
|------|-------|------|-------|
|      |       |      | 1NT   |
| Pass | 3NT   | End  |       |

South opens with a 15–17 point 1NT and is raised to game. Your partner, West, leads the ♠8 and declarer plays low from dummy. Sitting East, you pause to make a plan for the defence. Your partner would not have led the ♠8 from ♠Q–10–9–8, so the opening lead must be his second-best spade from a weak suit. Declarer is therefore marked with the queen and ten of spades. You win with the ♠A and must decide what to do next.

If you follow the general guideline to "lead up to weakness in the dummy", switching to the ♦10, declarer will easily make the contract. Before making such a play, you should count the points that are out.

You hold 10 points and there are 11 in the dummy. This leaves only 19 points for the two closed hands, of which South must hold at least 15. So, your partner can hold at most one high card in diamonds. What is more, declarer will have to play on diamonds himself, to stand any chance of scoring nine tricks.

Having worked this out, you should switch to a low heart – into the teeth of dummy's ♥K–J–6. It may seem strange to lead into strength in this way, but see the effect of it. When declarer wins the heart switch and plays a diamond, your partner wins with the ace and plays back a second round of hearts. You score three heart tricks and the game is defeated.

## Calculating which useful card partner may hold

By counting declarer's points, you can deduce how many points are left for your partner. Only a good player in the East seat would defeat this 3NT game:

**Right:** Calculating which useful card partner holds. By counting declarer's points, East determines which useful card it is possible for West to hold.

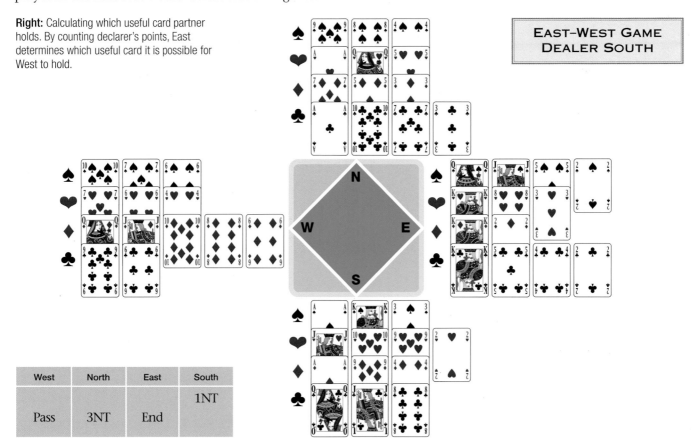

EAST–WEST GAME
DEALER SOUTH

| West | North | East | South |
|------|-------|------|-------|
|      |       |      | 1NT   |
| Pass | 3NT   | End  |       |

South opens a 15–17 point 1NT and is raised to game. Take the East cards now. West, your partner, leads the ♦Q and you must plan your defence. The first move is clear – you must overtake with the ♦K. Otherwise you risk blocking the suit. Declarer could then win the first trick and run the ♣Q to you, making the contract easily.

Declarer allows ♦K to win, breaking your link with partner's hand in diamonds. Many East players would now return their remaining diamond. It is not a strong defence. You can see 22 points between your hand and the dummy. Declarer is marked with at least 15 points for his 1NT opening, so your partner can hold no honour card outside his ♦Q–J. If you set up his diamonds, he will have no possible card of entry.

Once you have deduced that a diamond return cannot be successful, it is obvious that you should switch to a low spade. If partner holds ♠10–x–x, you will be able to set up two tricks in the suit before your remaining two kings are dislodged. Declarer wins the ♠2 switch with the

♠A and runs the jack of hearts to your king. You clear the spade suit and cash the setting tricks in spades when declarer takes a losing club finesse. If you returned a diamond instead, declarer would win with the ♦A and finesse in clubs. When you won with the ♣K, it would be too late to attack the spade suit. Declarer would win your spade switch and finesse in hearts, setting up enough tricks for the contract while he still held a spade stopper.

---

**CHINESE FINESSE**
♠ ♥ ♦ ♣

Suppose you need to avoid a loser with a side suit of ♦Q–9–8–3 opposite ♦A–5. If there is no possibility of an end-play of some sort, you may try the desperate manoeuvre of leading the ♦Q. When the player in the second seat holds something like ♦K–7–2, he may place you with ♦Q–J–10–x and thus decline to cover with the king. This deceptive play is known as a "Chinese Finesse".

---

# DEFENSIVE HOLD-UPS IN A SUIT CONTRACT

It is a familiar technique for the defenders to hold up an ace (or even a king), when defending in no-trumps. The same sort of move can work well against a suit contract too. The purpose, as always, will be to interfere with declarer's communications.

### Holding up to prevent declarer taking a discard
Take East cards on this deal and see how you get on.

**Right:** A hold-up to prevent a discard. East holds up the ◆A, to prevent declarer from obtaining a discard on the suit.

## COUNT SIGNALS
♠ ♥ ♦ ♣

By showing whether you hold an even or odd number of cards in a suit that declarer is playing (a high card shows "even", a low card shows "odd"), you can help your partner to judge when to hold up an ace in defence.

**GAME ALL**
**DEALER SOUTH**

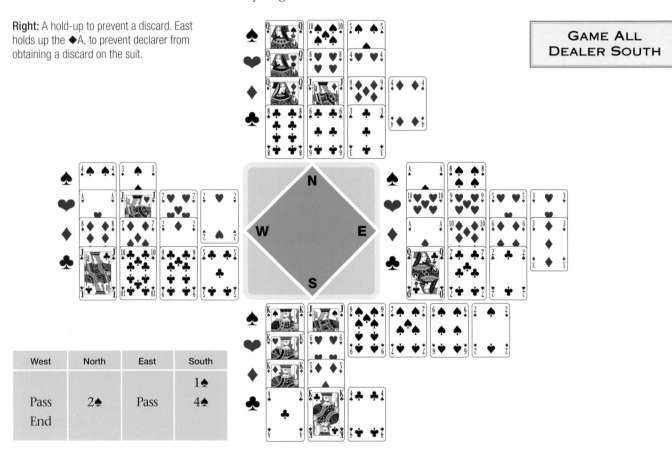

| West | North | East | South |
|------|-------|------|-------|
|      |       |      | 1♠    |
| Pass | 2♠    | Pass | 4♠    |
| End  |       |      |       |

West leads the ♣J. South wins with the ♣A and plays the ◆K from his hand. Sitting East, you must decide whether to win with the ◆A or to hold up the card. Suppose first that you do win the ace immediately, returning a club. This will be very much to declarer's liking. He will win the club return with the king and cross to dummy with the ◆Q. He can then throw his club loser on the ◆J. He will make the game, losing tricks only to the three aces.

When the ◆K is led, West will give a "count signal". A high diamond will indicate an even number of cards in the suit; a low diamond will show an odd number.

Here he will play the ◆2. Sitting East, you can then place West with three diamonds and declarer with two. On that basis you should hold up the ◆A on the first round. You win the second diamond and clear the club suit. Declarer has no quick entry to dummy, to take a discard on the ◆J, and will now go down. When he plays a trump to the queen, you will win with the ace and cash a club winner, followed by a heart to West's ace.

Suppose instead that West held ◆8–7–5–2. He would signal his count with the ◆7 (second highest from four cards). East would then take his ◆A immediately, preventing declarer from scoring the singleton ◆K.

## Holding up to prevent declarer taking a finesse

Sometimes a hold-up will keep declarer out of dummy, preventing him from taking a finesse through your hand.

**Right:** A hold-up to prevent a trump finesse. East holds up the ♦A to prevent declarer from entering dummy with the ♦Q to finesse in trumps.

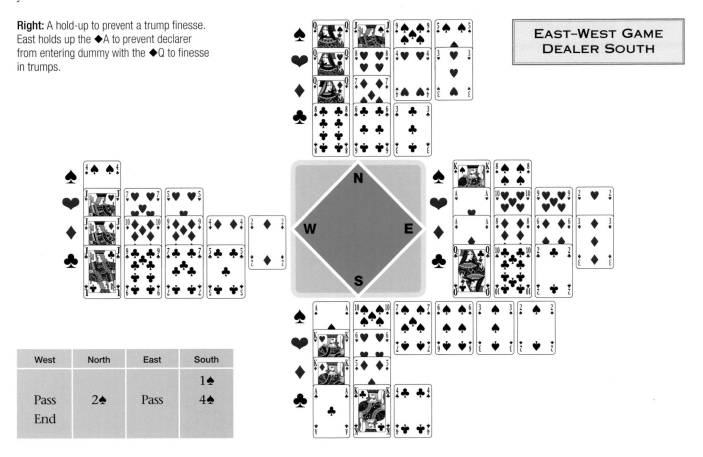

| | | | |
|---|---|---|---|
| **EAST–WEST GAME** | | | |
| **DEALER SOUTH** | | | |

| West | North | East | South |
|------|-------|------|-------|
| | | | 1♠ |
| Pass | 2♠ | Pass | 4♠ |
| End | | | |

West leads the ♦J and declarer plays low from dummy. You must consider your defence from the East seat. If you rise with the ♦A, declarer will unblock the ♦K from his hand and subsequently enter dummy with the ♦Q to finesse against your king of trumps. You should therefore play low at Trick 1. Another reason to play low is that you do not want declarer to score two diamond tricks (throwing a club from dummy on the third round of the suit) if he began with ♦K–x–x.

Declarer wins the first trick with ♦K and immediately leads the ♥K. Your partner follows with the ♥5, his lowest card in the suit showing an odd number of cards in the suit. You must hold up the ♥A, to prevent declarer from crossing to the ♥Q to take a trump finesse. After this bright start to the defence, declarer cannot reach dummy and will not be able to finesse against your ♠K. He will have to cash the ♠A from his hand. He cannot avoid a loser in every suit, as the cards lie, and will go one down.

### RULE OF FIFTEEN
♠ ♥ ♦ ♣

When you are short in spades, it is somewhat risky to make a light opening bid in the fourth seat. The defenders may then discover a spade fit and end in a successful part score (or even a game) in that suit, when you could have passed the deal out. Some players use the "Rule of Fifteen" to decide whether to open: *When the sum of your high-card points and the number of spades in your hand is 15 or more, you should open the bidding.* Suppose, after three passes, your hand is :

♠3 ♥A–J–9–8–4 ♦K–Q–8–4 ♣ Q–10–5.

You have 12 points and only 1 spade. According to the Rule of Fifteen, you should pass rather than opening 1♥. In any of the first three seats this hand would be worth an opening bid. The Rule of Fifteen applies only in the fourth seat.

# THE FORCING DEFENCE

When you hold four trumps in defence, it is often best to lead your strongest side suit. Your aim is to force declarer to ruff, thereby weakening his trump holding. If you can end with more trumps than declarer, he will have lost trump control and may well go down.

## Playing a forcing defence

West holds four trumps, defending this spade game, and therefore leads from his powerful heart side suit. His ♥K wins the first trick, and he continues with a low heart to East's ♥10.

**Right:** A typical forcing defence. By continually leading hearts, West forces declarer to lose control of the trump suit.

---

### MULTIPLE MEANING
### ♠ ♥ ♦ ♣

Many bridge words, such as "forcing" here, have more than one meaning within the game. A "forcing bid" is one that partner is not allowed to pass. A "forcing defence" describes the situation where the defenders force declarer to ruff, in order to weaken his trump holding. Also a defender might play a king, "forcing out dummy's ace".

---

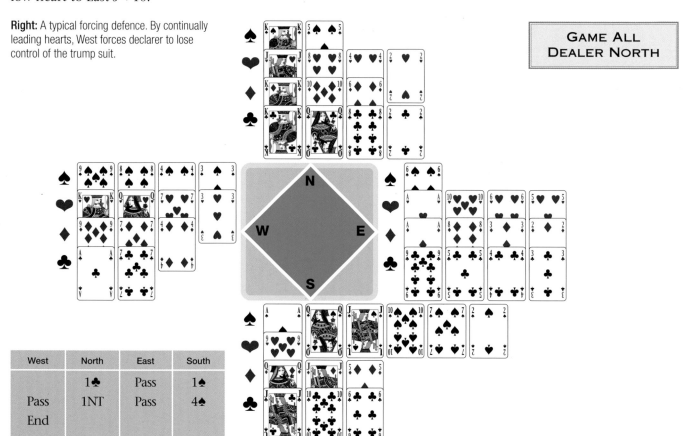

**GAME ALL
DEALER NORTH**

| West | North | East | South |
|------|-------|------|-------|
|      | 1♣    | Pass | 1♠    |
| Pass | 1NT   | Pass | 4♠    |
| End  |       |      |       |

Declarer ruffs and now holds five trumps to West's four. He plays two rounds of trumps and discovers the 4–1 break. Suppose he draws West's last two trumps and then plays on clubs. West will win with the ♣A and force declarer's last trump with a third round of hearts. Declarer can score three club tricks, but this will bring his total only to nine tricks. When he eventually plays on diamonds, East will win and the defenders will score a heart trick to beat the

contract. The outcome will be exactly the same if declarer plays on clubs before drawing West's last two trumps. Another heart will reduce him to just two trump winners and he will not be able to set up and enjoy a diamond trick.

Even though South began with six trumps to West's four, the force was successful. That is because declarer needed to dislodge two high cards and the defenders would have two more chances to force him.

## Holding up the trump ace to maintain the force

Suppose you are conducting a forcing defence and you hold four trumps headed by the ace. You will often have to hold up the ace until the trumps in declarer's shorter holding (usually the dummy's trumps) are exhausted. You can then persist with your force on the longer trump holding. The deal below is an example of this technique:

**Right:** Taking the trump ace at the right moment. By holding up the ace of trumps, West is able to continue his forcing defence.

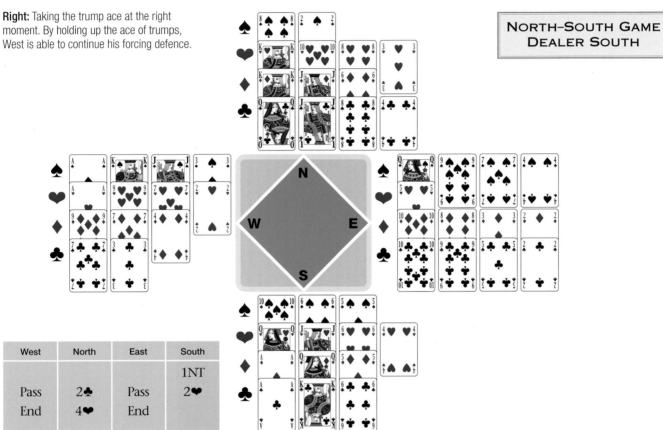

NORTH-SOUTH GAME
DEALER SOUTH

| West | North | East | South |
|------|-------|------|-------|
|      |       |      | 1NT   |
| Pass | 2♣    | Pass | 2♥    |
| End  | 4♥    | End  |       |

West leads the ♠A against South's heart game and the defenders play two more rounds of spades, forcing the dummy to ruff. When declarer leads the king of trumps from dummy, the key moment of the hand has been reached. If West makes the mistake of winning this round of trumps, he will not be able to persist with his forcing defence. That's because a fourth round of spades could be ruffed in dummy, in what has now become the shorter trump holding. Instead West should duck not only the first round of trumps but also the second round.

If declarer continues with a third round of trumps, dummy will have no trumps left. West will be able to win with the ♥A and force declarer's last trump with another spade, setting up his ♥9 as the setting trick. Declarer's only alternative is to abandon trumps after two rounds and to turn to the side suits. West will then ruff the third round of clubs, again scoring two trump tricks to beat the game. In the common situation where declarer has four trumps in each hand, you need to attack the trump length in both hands. The idea is to reduce the trump length in one hand, hold up the ace of trumps until that hand has no trumps remaining and then attack the trump length in the other hand.

**Above:** Dummy's trumps have been forced once already. West now holds up the ace of trumps twice, planning to win the third round and force out declarer's last trump with another spade.

# UNBLOCKING HONOURS IN DEFENCE

A ny time that you have a doubleton honour in a side suit, you must consider playing the honour on the first round. Failure to do this can cost you in various ways. You may block your partner's long suit, for example. You may also leave yourself open to an end-play by the declarer.

## Unblocking an honour in partner's suit

When you hold a doubleton honour in the suit that partner has led against no-trumps, it is generally right to play it on the first round, even if this is not necessary in an attempt to win the trick. Take the East cards here:

**Above:** East unblocks the ♠K on his partner's ♠Q lead. If he fails to do so, he will win the second round and be unable to continue the suit.

**Right:** Unblocking in the suit led. West leads the ♠Q against 3NT and East must play the ♠K to avoid the suit becoming blocked.

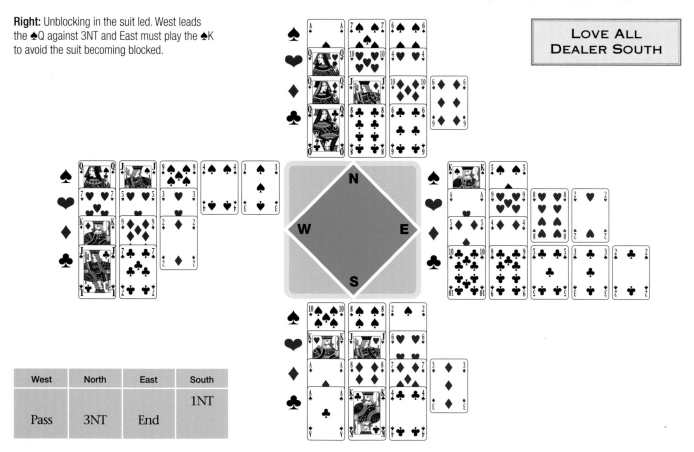

| | | | LOVE ALL DEALER SOUTH |

| West | North | East | South |
|------|-------|------|-------|
| | | | 1NT |
| Pass | 3NT | End | |

Your partner leads the ♠Q and declarer plays low from the dummy. It is essential you unblock your ♠K on the first round. You then return the ♠5, clearing the suit whether your partner has led from ♠Q–J–10–x–x or ♠Q–J–9–x–x. Declarer must take a diamond finesse at some stage. Your partner will win with the king and cash his spade winners. Four spades, the king of diamonds and the ace of hearts puts the contract two down.

Suppose instead that you fail to unblock, following with the ♠5. Declarer will duck the second round of spades and you will have to win with the bare ♠K. With his spade stopper intact, declarer will easily make the contract.

You would make the same unblocking play of the king if declarer played the ♠A from dummy at Trick 1, or if dummy had held ♠7–6–2.

## Unblocking to avoid an end-play

When declarer holds plenty of trumps in both hands, you must be particularly careful not to leave yourself with a bare honour in a side suit. If you do, you may be thrown in with the card and forced to give declarer a ruff-and-discard. Take the West cards here:

**Right:** Unblocking to avoid an end-play. When declarer plays the ◆A, West must unblock the ◆K to avoid being end-played later.

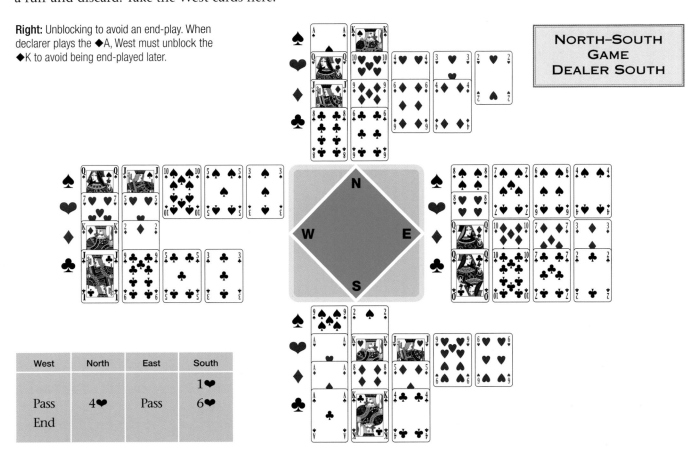

NORTH–SOUTH
GAME
DEALER SOUTH

| West | North | East | South |
|------|-------|------|-------|
|      |       |      | 1♥    |
| Pass | 4♥    | Pass | 6♥    |
| End  |       |      |       |

**Above:** World Grand Master Catherine D'Ovidio, shown on the extreme right of the French national team, has ranked World's top female player.

Sitting West, you lead the ♠Q against the slam. Declarer wins in the dummy, draws trumps in two rounds and cashes the ◆A. Suppose you see no need for special action and follow with the ◆2. Declarer will cash dummy's other spade winner, followed by the two high clubs in his hand and a club ruff. With the black suits eliminated, he will then play a second round of diamonds. You will have to win with the bare ◆K and return a black suit, conceding a ruff-and-discard. Declarer will ruff in the dummy, throwing the last diamond loser from his hand. Sadly for you and your partner, 12 tricks will then be his.

Difficult as it may seem, you must play your ◆K under South's ◆A. Your partner will then be able to win two diamond tricks. If declarer held the ◆Q or the ◆10, he would doubtless have finessed in the suit, rather than cashing the diamond ace.

# BREAKING DECLARER'S COMMUNICATIONS

Attractive as it may be for the defenders to set up extra tricks for themselves, sometimes this has to take second place behind the need to disrupt declarer's communications. Before you automatically "return partner's suit", you should take a look around and see if you can destroy an important entry to the dummy.

### Killing an entry to dummy

Take the East cards here and see how you would defend this 3NT contract. Your partner leads the ♠2 and you win with the ace.

**Right:** Killing the entry to dummy. East wins the spade lead against 3NT and must switch to hearts to kill the entry to dummy's diamonds.

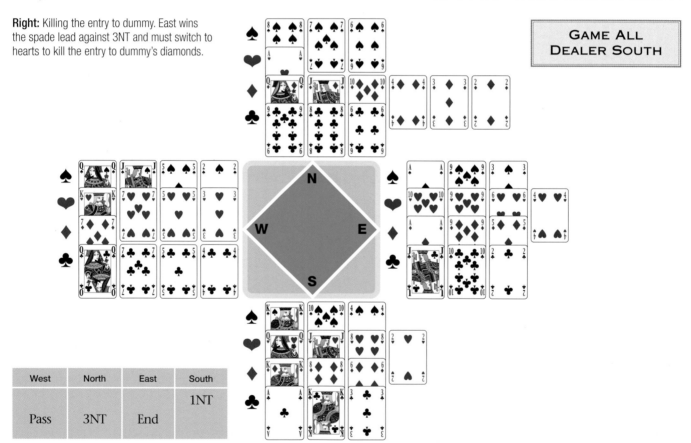

**GAME ALL
DEALER SOUTH**

| West | North | East | South |
|------|-------|------|-------|
|      |       |      | 1NT   |
| Pass | 3NT   | End  |       |

Suppose you follow your natural instincts and return the ♠9. Declarer will win with the king and lead the ♦K. It will not do you any good to hold up the diamond ace for a couple of rounds because the ace of hearts is still intact as an entry to dummy. The defenders can score three spades and a diamond but declarer will then score five diamonds and the four top winners in the other three suits, making the no-trump game.

At Trick 2 your top priority, sitting East, is to kill declarer's source of tricks in dummy's diamond suit by removing the heart entry to dummy. You should switch to a heart, won by dummy's ace. The job of cutting declarer off from his diamond winners is only half done. When he plays on diamonds, you must hold up the ace until the third round. Declarer will then make two diamond tricks, rather than five, and will go two down.

## The Merrimac Coup

As we have just seen, it is easy enough to dislodge a bare ace from dummy. When the ace is guarded, something more spectacular may be required. Take the East cards here:

**Right:** A spectacular sacrifice. East notes that dummy's diamonds are threatening and sacrifices his ♠K to remove the ♠A entry to the dummy.

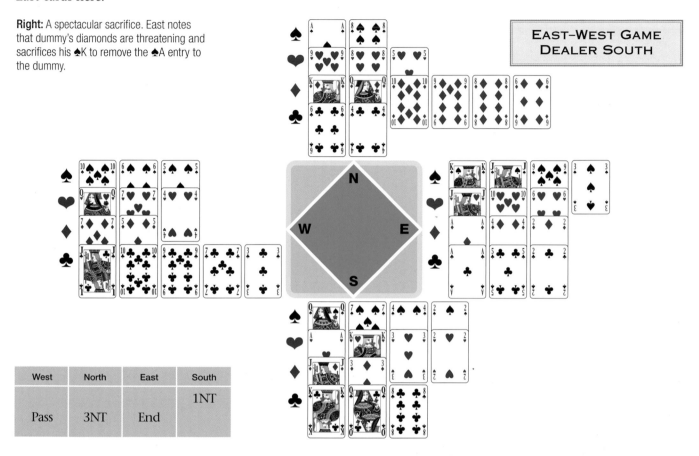

EAST–WEST GAME
DEALER SOUTH

| West | North | East | South |
|------|-------|------|-------|
|      |       |      | 1NT   |
| Pass | 3NT   | End  |       |

West leads the ♣J and you must plan the defence from the East seat. There are only 18 points missing from the West and South hands. West has already shown the ♣J, so declarer is marked with the ♣K as well as the ♣Q.

If you play low at Trick 1, declarer will win and clear the diamond suit while the ♠A is intact as an entry. He will make the contract with an overtrick, however you defend thereafter. Instead you must rise smartly with the club ace and attack the spade entry to dummy. Switching to a low spade will not be good enough, as the cards lie, because declarer will be able to win with the spade queen. The only winning defence is to switch to the ♠K! Declarer has no answer to this. If he wins with dummy's ace, you will subsequently hold up your ♦A to cut him off from the diamond suit. If instead declarer allows your ♠K to win, you will continue with a low spade, removing dummy's side entry. Either way, the contract will go at least one down.

**Above:** The Merrimac Coup, a sacrificial play, is named after the deliberate scuttling of the American coal-carrying ship, *Merrimac*, in Santiago Harbour in 1898. The aim was to bottle up the Spanish fleet.

# PROMOTING TRUMP TRICKS IN DEFENCE

Few things are more enjoyable in defence than promoting extra trump tricks. You can do this in two different ways. The first is to lead a suit where declarer (or the dummy) is now void and your partner is in a position to overruff. If declarer chooses to ruff low, your partner will indeed overruff. If instead declarer ruffs high, this may promote a trump trick for one or other of the defenders. The second promotion technique is known as the "uppercut". A defender ruffs with a high trump, aiming to force declarer to overruff with a higher trump. The intention is to promote some lesser trump in the other defender's hand.

## The trump promotion

The deal below shows an example of the basic form of trump promotion where one defender is in a position to overruff the declarer.

East opens with a weak two-bid in spades and South arrives in 4♥. West leads the ♠9 and East wins with the ♠J. He cashes the ♠A and then leads a third round of spades in the hope that this will achieve a trump promotion. If declarer ruffs with the ♥9, West will overruff with the ♥10 and the trump ace will give the defenders a fourth trick for one down. Since declarer knows from the bidding that the spades are breaking 6–2, he may well ruff with the ♥K instead.

All will now depend on West's reaction. If he succumbs to the temptation to overruff with the ♥A, the contract will survive. When declarer regains the lead, he will draw West's remaining two trumps with the queen and jack. West should decline to overruff, discarding a diamond instead. His ♥A–10–4 will then be worth two tricks, sitting over South's ♥Q–J–9–7–2. The third round of spades will have promoted an extra trump trick in the West hand. West will score both the ace and the ten of the suit.

Suppose West had held ♥A–9–4 instead of ♥A–10–4. Again it would be right to decline to overruff. By defending in this way, he would promote a second trump trick when his partner held the ♥10.

**Right:** A typical trump promotion. West leads the ♠9 against the heart game and East plays three rounds of the suit for a trump promotion.

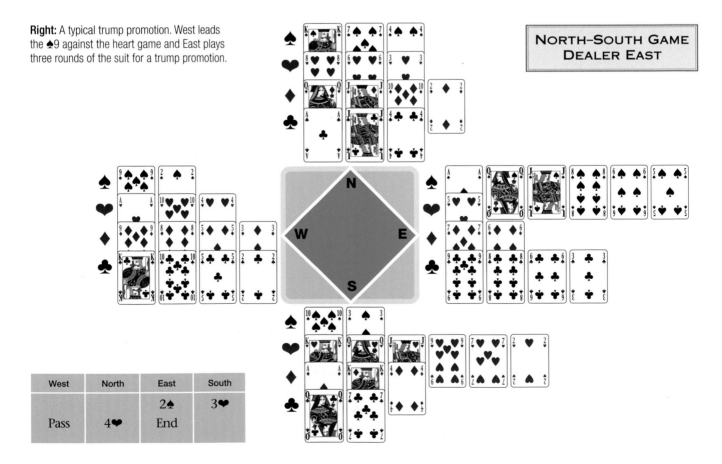

NORTH–SOUTH GAME
DEALER EAST

| West | North | East | South |
|------|-------|------|-------|
|      |       | 2♠   | 3♥    |
| Pass | 4♥    | End  |       |

## The uppercut

You can also promote a trump trick by ruffing high when you expect to be overruffed:

**Right:** An uppercut. East defeats the spade game by administering an uppercut, ruffing with the ♠Q on the fourth round of hearts.

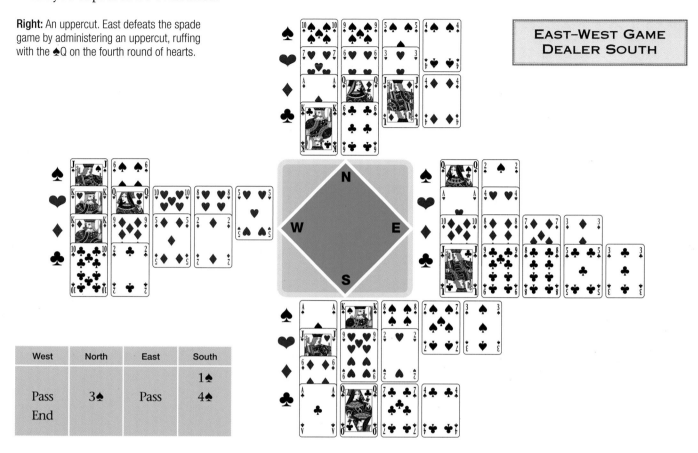

| | EAST–WEST GAME DEALER SOUTH |
|---|---|

| West | North | East | South |
|------|-------|------|-------|
| | | | 1♠ |
| Pass | 3♠ | Pass | 4♠ |
| End | | | |

West leads the ♥K. If East follows with the ♥4, an overtrick will be made. He will have to win the next heart with the bare ace and that is the last trick that the defenders will take.

Instead, East overtakes with the ♥A and returns the ♥4. West scores the ten and queen of the suit, giving the defenders the first three tricks. On the third round of hearts East discards the ♣3, showing no interest in that suit. With his ◆K sitting under the dummy's ◆A–Q–J, West can see no prospect of a minor-suit trick for the defence. The only chance is to promote a trump trick. West continues with a fourth round of hearts and East ruffs with the ♠Q (a play known as an uppercut). Declarer overruffs with the king or ace and now has to lose a trick to West's ♠J. The game goes one down. The same defence would have been successful if East had started with a singleton ♠Q, or a singleton or doubleton ♠K.

---

### MOST PROLIFIC BRIDGE WRITERS
♠ ♥ ◆ ♣

The world's top bridge writers (in terms of the number of books written) are:

1. Terence Reese (England)
2. David Bird (England)
3. Ron Klinger (Australia)
4. Hugh Kelsey (Scotland)
5. Brian Senior (England)
6. Ely Culbertson (USA)
7. Victor Mollo (England)
8. Eddie Kantar (USA)
9. Charles Goren (USA)
10. Danny Kleinman (USA)

**Above:** David Bird and Terence Reese, who have written the greatest number of books about bridge.

# CHAPTER 7

# FAMOUS PLAYERS

Every game or sport has its larger than life characters, who catch the public eye and are remembered for decades. Bridge is no exception. It is largely a game for extroverts and this section pays homage to some of the outstanding figures who have spent their lives gracing the bridge table. Film star Omar Sharif is perhaps the most well-known bridge player in the world. Robert Hamman and Jeff Meckstroth of the USA, Gabriel Chagas of Brazil and Zia Mahmood of Pakistan (now of the USA) are all currently playing at the top level. Maestro Benito Garozzo, star of the fabulous Italian Blue Team, still plays bridge on the Internet. The other three players described in this section are no longer alive – the great player and writer, Terence Reese of England, and two of the finest women players of all time: USA's Helen Sobel and Rixi Markus of Austria (later of England).

**Right:** Omar Sharif plays a tense game of bridge with some of the world's best players as part of a televised competition in Mayfair, London, in 1970. The opponent to his right is Jonathan Cansino of England.

## GABRIEL CHAGAS (BRAZIL)

Gabriel Chagas is by far the most successful bridge player to emerge from South America. Since 1968, he has won the South American championship 22 times and the Brazilian championship 24 times. He has also represented Brazil in more than 40 world championship events. He is one of only eight players ever to have won bridge's Triple Crown: the Olympiad, the Bermuda Bowl and the World Pairs. A company director living in Rio de Janeiro, Chagas speaks eight languages fluently and can communicate well in several others. He is also proficient at tennis, sings and plays the piano.

Here is a brilliant deceptive defence of his, from the 1995 Rio Teams Championship. Chagas was East on the deal shown below. North had promised a four-card major, by using the Stayman convention, and his subsequent 3NT denied four cards in the heart suit. Deducing that there was a 4-4 spade fit, South bid 4♠ over his partner's 3NT.

Following the scheme popular in the USA, West led the ♣2 from his holding of three small cards. Chagas could see 25 points between his own hand and the dummy. South's 1NT bid had promised 15–17 points, so Chagas knew every honour card in declarer's hand. Suppose East wins with the ♣J and switches to a diamond at Trick 2. Declarer will have no alternative but to finesse the ♦J. This will succeed and he will make the game easily. He will draw trumps, play the ♦A and lead a club to the 10. After scoring two club tricks, East would be end-played, forced to lead a heart into dummy's tenace or to concede a ruff-and-discard.

Chagas decided to put up a smoke screen. Pretending that he held ♣A–J doubleton, he cashed the club ace at Trick 2. He then switched to the ♦9. How could declarer possibly take the finesse now? If it lost, West would surely give his partner a club ruff and beat the contract. Barbosa duly rose with the ♦A, drew trumps and took what he assumed was the guaranteed finesse of the ♣10, to set up a discard for his diamond loser. We can only imagine his reaction when the club finesse lost to the ♣Q and Chagas proceeded to cash the ♦K.

**Right:** A brilliant deceptive defence. Chagas disguises his club holding to persuade declarer not to finesse in diamonds.

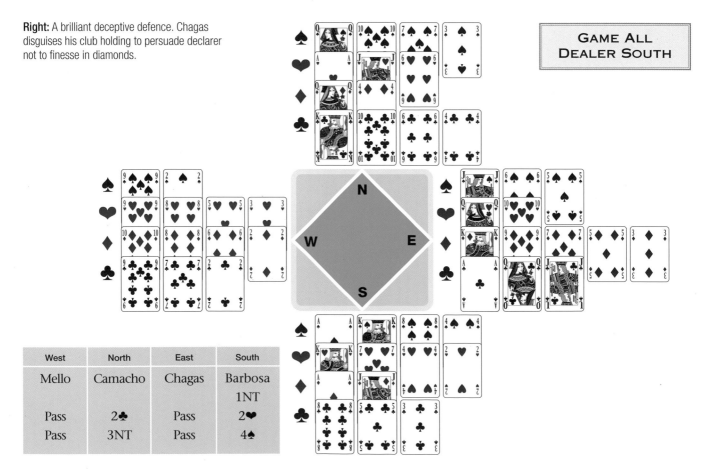

GAME ALL
DEALER SOUTH

| West | North | East | South |
|------|-------|------|-------|
| Mello | Camacho | Chagas | Barbosa |
| | | | 1NT |
| Pass | 2♣ | Pass | 2♥ |
| Pass | 3NT | Pass | 4♠ |

# BENITO GAROZZO (ITALY)

Benito Garozzo was born in Naples in 1927. He learnt to play bridge with some friends during World War II (1939–45). Amazingly he attributes his early fascination with card combinations to Autobridge. (Autobridge was a teaching aid, containing hands set by Culbertson. The player had to slide open small windows in a plastic box to reveal the cards.) By 1954 Garozzo was playing with the top players in Italy and he eventually became a leading light in what was perhaps the greatest bridge team ever – the Italian Blue Team. His list of partners includes many of Italy's finest players. From 1961–72 he played with Pietro Forquet. Then, from 1972 for three years he joined forces with the fiery Giorgio Belladonna. Arturo Franco and Lorenzo Lauria were his next partners, each for a two-year period, and from 1982–5 he rejoined Belladonna. Throughout these years the Blue Team was almost unbeatable. Garozzo won the Bermuda Bowl ten times and the World Teams Olympiad three times. From the time of his first

**Above:** Garozzo considers his next move.

Bermuda Bowl win in 1961, he never played in a losing team in international competition until 1976, an incomparable record of excellence.

Garozzo rates as his finest performance the closing stages of the 1975 Bermuda Bowl in Bermuda. The Italian team had been forced to withdraw one of their three pairs, after an allegation of passing signals via foot-tapping. The remaining two pairs therefore had to play throughout, which was exhausting. At one stage in the final they were 70 IMPs behind a very strong American team. Amazingly they fought their way back to win.

Here is a fine deceptive play, made by Garozzo during the 1975 Italian Open Teams.

**Right:** An imaginative deceptive play. By ducking a trick that he could have won, Garozzo misleads the defender and makes an "impossible" game.

NORTH–SOUTH GAME
DEALER WEST

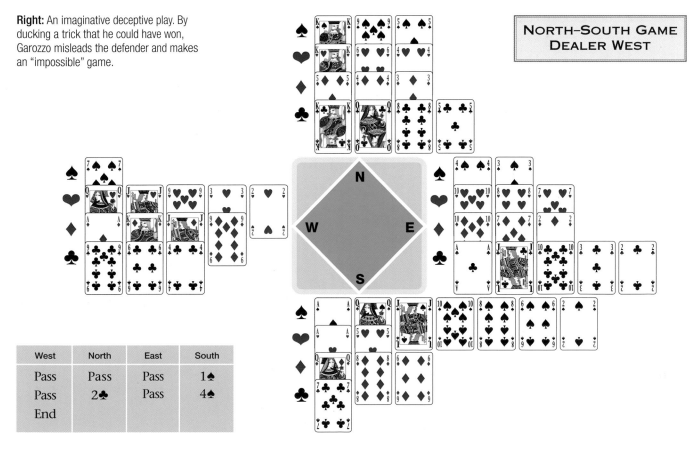

| West | North | East | South |
|------|-------|------|-------|
| Pass | Pass | Pass | 1♠ |
| Pass | 2♣ | Pass | 4♠ |
| End | | | |

Most players would open on the West cards nowadays and a surprising number would open on the North cards too. As it was, Garozzo opened 1♠ in the fourth seat and leapt to game in spades when Belladonna responded at the two-level.

West led the ♦K and received a discouraging signal from his partner. He then switched to the ♥Q. Garozzo had a fair idea how the cards must lie. West had indicated the ♦A–K with his opening lead and had also shown at least two points in hearts. If he held the ♣A in addition he would have 13 points, enough to open the bidding. It was therefore certain that East held the ♣A. If declarer played in straightforward fashion, drawing trumps and trying to establish a diamond discard on dummy's clubs, East would win the first round of clubs and sink the contract by switching back to diamonds.

Rather than accept defeat, Garozzo made the brilliant deceptive play of allowing the ♥Q to win! A club switch, followed by a return to diamonds, would now have put the game two down. West naturally assumed that his partner held the ♥A, however. He continued with a second round of hearts and the contract was home. Garozzo unmasked his deception, winning with the ♥A, and then drew trumps in two rounds, ending in the dummy. He discarded his singleton club on the ♥K and led the ♣K for a ruffing finesse. When East covered with the ace, he ruffed in the South hand and returned to dummy with a trump to discard one of his diamonds on the established ♣Q. He had made the seemingly impossible game.

In these days of full-time professional players, it is an interesting reminder of times gone by that Garozzo had another professional "day job" throughout his great bridge career – he owned a jewellery store in Naples, Italy. He now lives in California, USA, where he plays bridge frequently on the Internet, and is also found at the table with Lea DuPont. In both cases you can be sure that an army of admirers will be following his every move.

# ROBERT HAMMAN (USA)

Robert Hamman became the world's top-ranked player in 1985 and retained that status for an amazing 20 years. He has won an unparalleled number of North American titles, the 1988 Olympiad, and the Bermuda Bowl an almost unbelievable nine times (1970, 1971, 1977, 1983, 1985, 1987, 1995, 1999 and 2003). He also won the World Open Pairs championship with Bobby Wolff in 1974. Unlike most of the USA's top players, Hamman achieved all this success while performing an important job outside the game – he was president of SCA Promotions, a prize promotion company.

Hamman joined Ira Corn's Dallas Aces team in 1969, initially partnering Eddie Kantar. He went on to partner Mike Lawrence, Paul Soloway, Billy Eisenberg and Don Krauss, before forming a 25-year-long partnership with Bobby Wolff. His wife, Petra, won the Venice Cup in 2000.

Here is a fine play by Hamman, from USA's win in the final of the 1970 Bermuda Bowl. The Chinese West led the ♠K and Hamman allowed this card to win.

**Above:** Robert Hamman, playing in the 1973 World Bridge Championship at the Casa Grande Hotel in Guaruja, Brazil. The USA team reached the final but were defeated by Italy.

He took the next round of spades and now had to set up a diamond discard on the club suit. It was not just a question of finding clubs 3–3 with the ace onside, because the defenders might be able to establish their diamond trick before declarer could enjoy his discard.

At Trick 2 Hamman led the ♣7 from his hand. Suppose West were to rise with the ♣A now and switch to a diamond. East's ♦10 would force the ♦A, yes, but declarer could then run the ♦9 to establish a discard for his remaining club loser. West in fact played low on the first round of clubs and Hamman played accurately by passing the trick to East's ♣10. East, who could not attack diamonds successfully from his side of the table, returned another spade. Hamman ruffed and drew trumps with the king and queen. He could then lead a second round of clubs towards the king, setting up the discard that he needed whether West took his ♣A now or on the second round. (If trumps had broken 3–1, the ♥A would have served as an entry to the long clubs.)

As the cards lay, West could have defeated the game with the amazing play of the ♣J on the first round! If declarer wins with dummy's ♣K, West can win the second round of clubs with the ♣A and clear a

**Above:** The USA win the 1983 Bermuda Bowl in Stockholm. Hamman is shown with team-mates Ron Rubin, Bobby Wolff and Peter Weichsel.

diamond trick. If instead declarer ducks in the dummy, West can switch to a diamond then, with two club tricks guaranteed.

**Right:** Clever play justifies a bold bid. By ducking the first round of clubs, Hamman avoids a damaging diamond switch.

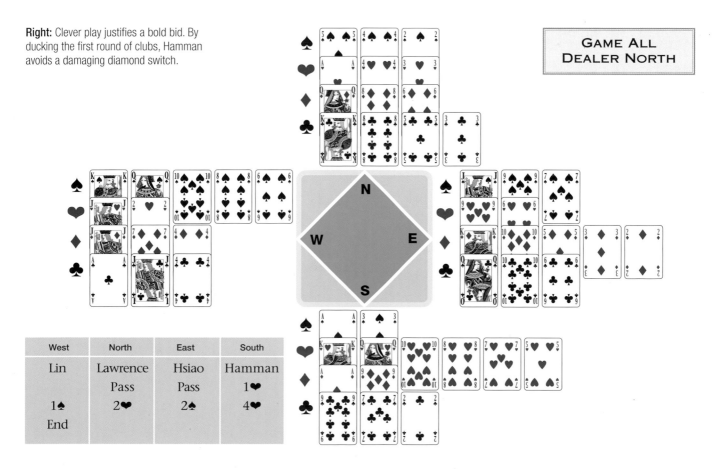

GAME ALL
DEALER NORTH

| West | North | East | South |
|------|-------|------|-------|
| Lin | Lawrence | Hsiao | Hamman |
| | Pass | Pass | 1♥ |
| 1♠ | 2♥ | 2♠ | 4♥ |
| End | | | |

# Zia Mahmood (Pakistan/USA)

Zia is one of the most colourful and skilful players in the game today. If you enter the playing area of a tournament where he is competing, you can easily find his table. It will be the one with the greatest number of spectators (a large proportion of them female). Born into a wealthy family in Pakistan, he represented his home country with great distinction. The highlight was in 1981 when Pakistan exceeded all expectation by reaching the final of the Bermuda Bowl, eventually losing to the USA.

Zia did not learn bridge until he was 25. At that time a beautiful woman invited him to play with her that evening at the local club. "You do know how to play, don't you?" she said. "Of course," Zia replied. He spent the afternoon studying *Five Weeks to Winning Bridge* by Alfred Sheinwold, but was nevertheless exposed as a completely hopeless player in the evening bridge session. Zia soon lost interest in the woman but became addicted to the game of bridge and could not learn quickly enough.

Nowadays Zia has homes in London and New York and represents the USA at bridge. On his first major appearance for an American team he persuaded his team-mates to wear Pakistani costume, to quell any guilt he might have had on switching allegiance. Zia's regular partner is Michael Rosenberg, formerly of Scotland but now also representing the USA. Zia and Rosenberg finished 2nd in the 2002 World Open Pairs in Montreal.

In 1990, in Atlantic City, Zia won the Omar Sharif World Individual Championship, where players are required to partner every other player for one round and a fixed bidding system is played. The event carried a $40,000 first prize. By winning the 2004 World Transnational Teams Championship in Istanbul, Zia acquired the coveted rank of World Grandmaster.

Shown below is a big deal from the semi-final of the 1981 Bermuda Bowl – contested in Port Chester, New York – with Pakistan sitting in the North–South seats and facing Argentina:

### GAME ALL
### DEALER SOUTH

**Below:** A fine grand slam in the 1981 Bermuda Bowl. Zia establishes the heart suit to dispose of his diamond losers.

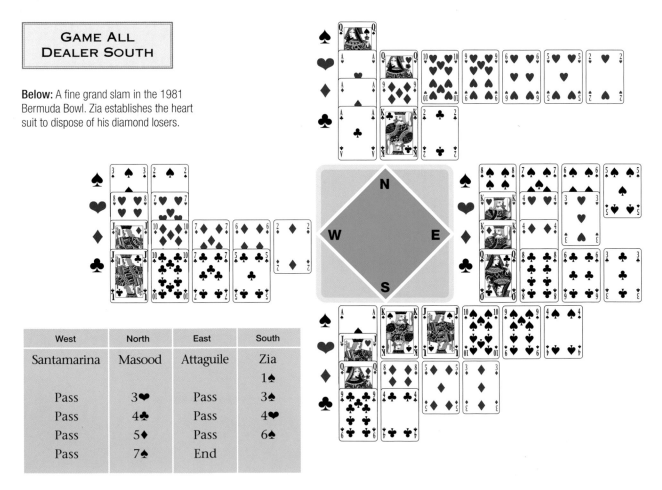

| West | North | East | South |
|------|-------|------|-------|
| Santamarina | Masood | Attaguile | Zia |
| | | | 1♠ |
| Pass | 3♥ | Pass | 3♠ |
| Pass | 4♣ | Pass | 4♥ |
| Pass | 5♦ | Pass | 6♠ |
| Pass | 7♠ | End | |

led the ♠Q to Trick 2, overtaking in his hand. After drawing trumps in four rounds, he led the ♥J to dummy's ♥A and ruffed a heart. When hearts broke 3–2, he was able to cross to dummy with a club and establish the heart suit with a further ruff. He could then return to the remaining club honour and enjoy the rest of the heart suit, claiming his grand slam. Pakistan went on to defeat Argentina, eventually losing to the USA in the final.

**Above:** Zia Mahmood is a great advocate of natural bidding, rather than artificial bidding – another reason why he is a favourite with kibitzers.

Zia's leap to 6♠ on the fourth round persuaded Masood that the trump suit would be solid. Trusting that the heart suit could be brought in, he raised to the grand slam. (At the other table, after the same first six bids, the Argentinian South bid only 5♠ and passed his partner's raise to 6♠.)

Zia went on to win the diamond lead with dummy's ace. He knew that to play on hearts immediately, ruffing the second round high, would lead to trouble if the trumps broke 5–1. Zia therefore

**Above:** Zia lent his strong support to the building of a school, to be known as the World Bridge School, in an earthquake-stricken part of Pakistan.

## RIXI MARKUS (AUSTRIA/ ENGLAND)

Rixi Markus was born in Austria and represented that country as they won the 1935 and 1936 European women's teams championships, followed by a win in the women's world championship in 1937 in Budapest. Driven to England in the war years, she formed a fearsome partnership with Fritzi Gordon, another émigré Austrian. At the time they were rated by many as the top women's pair in the

world. Rixi won another seven European Championships, now representing Great Britain. In 1962 she and Fritzi won both the World Women's Pairs and the World Mixed Teams, followed in 1964 by a win in the Women's Olympiad in New York. In 1974 the pair again won the World Women's Pairs, by a record margin. Rixi became the first female World Grandmaster. For her services to the game of bridge she was honoured by the Queen with the MBE.

A tiger at the bridge table, Rixi was charming socially and had countless friends around the world. Her bidding was undisciplined and she entered the auction in situations that would terrify a lesser personality. It was in the card play that she excelled.

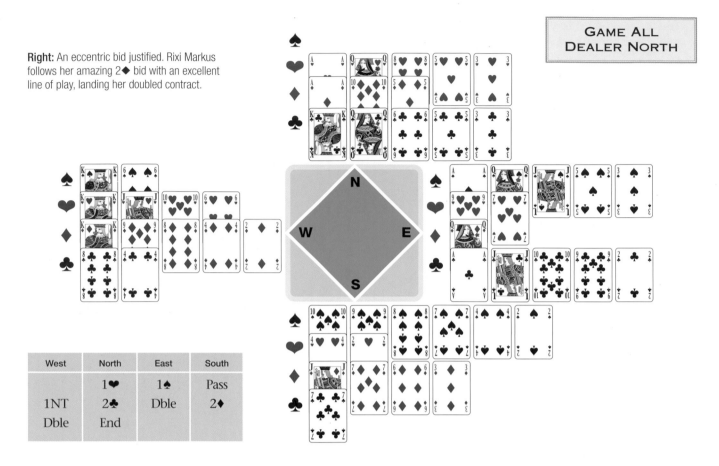

**Right:** An eccentric bid justified. Rixi Markus follows her amazing 2♦ bid with an excellent line of play, landing her doubled contract.

GAME ALL
DEALER NORTH

| West | North | East | South |
|------|-------|------|-------|
|      | 1♥    | 1♠   | Pass  |
| 1NT  | 2♣    | Dble | 2♦    |
| Dble | End   |      |       |

Above is a typical piece of Rixi action, taken from a rubber bridge game.

Expecting her partner to be void in spades, after the opponents' bidding, Rixi tried her luck in 2♦. West was happy to double this. He led the ♠K, which Rixi ruffed in the dummy. When she continued with the ♣K, East won with the ace and returned the ♦Q to dummy's ace. Some players now might cash the ♣Q, throwing a heart, and then score as many tricks as possible by ruffing hearts in hand and spades on the table.

Rixi realized that this line would bring her only seven tricks. Abandoning her established club trick, she ruffed a low club in her hand. She was then able to take the heart finesse, which was a near certainty on the bidding and the play so far. She then cashed the ♥A, ruffed a heart, ruffed a spade, ruffed a heart and ruffed another spade. In this way she scored two hearts and six trump tricks. She made the doubled contract exactly, without ever scoring her established second trick in clubs.

**Right:** Fritzi Gordon, long-time partner of Rixi Markus. She won the World Women's Teams in 1964, the World Women's Pairs in 1962 and 1974 and the World Mixed Teams in 1962.

# JEFF MECKSTROTH (USA)

Ask any top bridge player nowadays who they rate as the toughest opposition in the world and the likely answer is Jeff Meckstroth and Eric Rodwell of the USA. Meckstroth was a scratch golfer as a teenager. He learnt bridge before going to college, met Rodwell in 1974 and formed a partnership with him the following year. Together they have won almost everything worth winning in bridge – several Reisingers, Vanderbilts and Spingolds (the premier championships in the USA), the Macallan Invitational Pairs in 1995 and 1996, the World Team Olympiad in 1988 and the Bermuda Bowl in 1995, 1999 and 2003.

Meckstroth and Rodwell play a very scientific version of the Precision Club system, one that involves light opening bids. The printed description of their bidding system runs to two or three hundred pages. They are noted for their supreme temperament at the table, despite fiery reputations from their younger days. In 1992 they joined Robert Hamman and Robert Wolff to represent the Scientists against the Naturals in a £50,000 challenge match in London, winning by 70 IMPs.

The deal below features a supremely inventive piece of declarer play by Meckstroth, when facing the world class Norwegians, Geir Helgemo and Tor Helness.

South's 3♣ was a weak response, as the Americans play it. Rodwell rebid 3NT, the contract bid and made at the other table, but Meckstroth took another bid and ended in the apparently doomed club game.

Helness led a diamond and Meckstroth saw that there was little prospect in trying to set up the hearts for a spade discard. When he knocked out the first heart, the defenders would surely switch to spades, establishing a third trick for themselves there. To make life more difficult for his opponents, Meckstroth made the amazing play of the ♦10 from dummy! Helgemo won with the ♦Q and could see no pressing need to switch to hearts. He returned another diamond, on which Meckstroth discarded one of his hearts. The defenders could no longer beat the contract. A heart was played to the queen and ace and a spade switch would not now help the defenders. Declarer was subsequently able to take a ruffing finesse through East's ♥A, setting up a discard for his spade loser.

| | |
|---|---|
| **GAME ALL**<br>**DEALER NORTH** | |

**Below:** A brilliantly inventive deceptive play. Jeff Meckstroth surrenders an unnecessary diamond trick, causing the world-class defenders to go wrong.

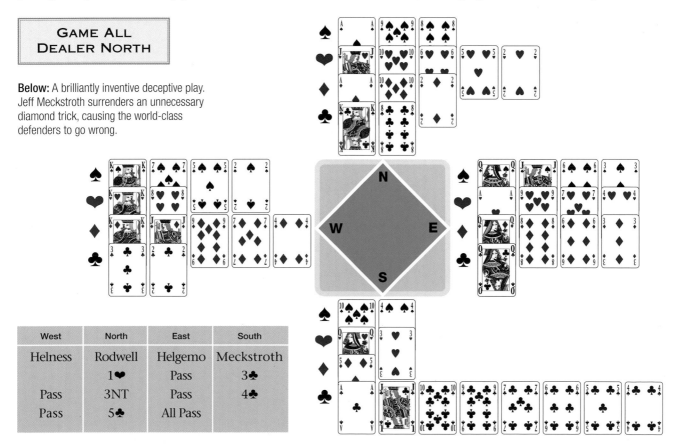

| West | North | East | South |
|---|---|---|---|
| Helness | Rodwell | Helgemo | Meckstroth |
| | 1♥ | Pass | 3♣ |
| Pass | 3NT | Pass | 4♣ |
| Pass | 5♣ | All Pass | |

# TERENCE REESE (ENGLAND)

There can be little doubt that Terence Reese is the greatest bridge writer there has ever been. He wrote 107 titles, which included several genuine masterpieces that were years ahead of their time: *The Expert Game*, *Reese on Play* and *Play Bridge with Reese*. He named various expert techniques, including the Crocodile Coup, the Dentist's Coup, the Vice Squeeze and the Winkle Squeeze. He also wrote eruditely on the Principle of Restricted Choice, which mystifies many players even today.

At his peak, Reese was rated by many as the best bridge player in the world. He formed an outstanding partnership with Boris Schapiro and won four European Championships, the 1955 Bermuda Bowl, the 1962 World Pairs championship and the 1961 World Pair championship (where very difficult hands are set for the players). On the domestic front, he won Britain's Gold Cup eight times and the Master Pairs seven times.

Reese's parents met when they were "First Gentleman" and "First Lady" at a whist drive. He learned to play cards before he could read and learnt Auction Bridge at the age of seven. He recounts in his autobiography *Bridge at the Top* how he had to dismount from his chair to sort his cards behind a cushion, 13 being somewhat of a handful.

Reese's career as a player was severely dented by a cheating allegation at the 1965 Bermuda Bowl in Buenos Aires. It was claimed that he and his partner Boris Schapiro had been using finger signals during the bidding, to inform their partner how many hearts they held. The pair was convicted by the World Bridge Federation but later acquitted by a special inquiry set up by the British Bridge League. Although photographs had been taken that showed unusual finger positions by the pair, there was remarkably little evidence from the records of the play of any advantage having been taken of the knowledge supposedly gained. To this day, players will dispute whether any cheating did in fact take place. Be that as it may, the partnership never played again in any international event.

**Below:** Press photographers await Reese and Schapiro on their return from Buenos Aires. The allegation of finger signalling was news across the world.

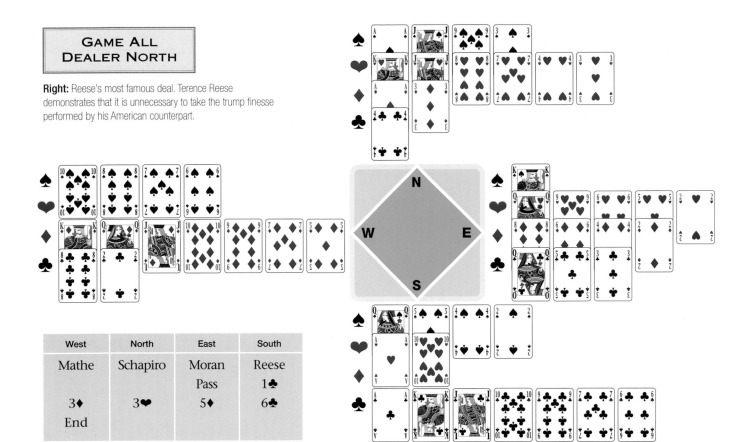

**GAME ALL
DEALER NORTH**

**Right:** Reese's most famous deal. Terence Reese demonstrates that it is unnecessary to take the trump finesse performed by his American counterpart.

| West | North | East | South |
|------|-------|------|-------|
| Mathe | Schapiro | Moran | Reese |
| | | Pass | 1♣ |
| 3♦ | 3♥ | 5♦ | 6♣ |
| End | | | |

The slam shown above is perhaps the most famous contract that Reese ever played.

A brief auction carried Reese to a small slam in clubs. West led the ♦9, rather than the normal top honour from a sequence, in the hope that East might win with the ♦A and deliver a heart ruff. Reese ruffed the opening lead and spurned the trump finesse, cashing the ace and king. When the ♣Q did not fall, he needed to set up dummy's heart suit to avoid losing a spade trick.

Reese played the ♥A, West showing out, and continued with a heart to the king and the ♥7, covered and ruffed. He then threw East on lead with the queen of trumps. Whatever card East played next, Reese would have enough entries to dummy to take a ruffing finesse in hearts and eventually enjoy the winners in the suit. He would be able to throw all his potential losers in spades.

At the other table, Rosen (for the USA) reached the same contract. He won the diamond lead with dummy's ace and took a successful trump finesse, making the slam easily. A flat board, yes, but he would have gone down if the trump finesse had lost to a doubleton queen with West. The superior line taken by Reese would be remembered for decades.

## PERFECT COMBINATION
♠ ♥ ♦ ♣

Many of the world's top bridge partnerships have consisted of one steady, technical player combined with a more flamboyant partner. A classic example of this was the long-standing partnership of Terence Reese and Boris Schapiro. Reese was a scholarly card-player but a somewhat cautious bidder. Schapiro was less accurate in the play and far more ambitious in the bidding. The pair won many championships, including a record number of Gold Cups.

**Above:** Boris Schapiro (left) was never afraid of displaying his emotions at the bridge table. His partnership with Terence Reese (right) lasted some 25 years.

## OMAR SHARIF (EGYPT)

Omar Sharif, the film actor who first came to public attention playing the role of Ali Ibn Kharish in *Lawrence of Arabia* (1962), has had a life-long fascination with the game of bridge. He captained the team representing the United Arab Republic in the 1964 Bridge Olympiad and by 1968 had formed an attachment with some of the best players in the world. A team known as the Omar Sharif Bridge Circus was formed, containing Delmouly and Yallouze of France, the incomparable Belladonna and Garozzo of Italy and Omar himself. They played a match in London, against England's Flint and Cansino, for the huge stakes (then) of £100 a 100. Sharif's team won handsomely but were generally thought to have had the better of the cards.

In 1975 Sharif's team toured the USA, playing 60-board matches against the champion teams of each region. They were sponsored by Lancia cars and any team that could beat them would win a red Lancia sports car each! The team's PR man, the famous tennis player Nicola Pietrangeli, did not enjoy phoning the sponsors in Rome no fewer than three times, to tell them that they should arrange the shipment of another set of cars.

**In his book** *Omar Sharif Talks Bridge*,
**Omar tells this story:**

Playing bridge and acting have one thing in common. When you are performing, your heart beats very much faster than normal. When I first started to play with members of the Italian Blue Team, they tended to frown every time I put down the dummy. This put a great strain on my heart. As often as not, all would turn out well in the end and the contract would be made. Meanwhile I had been suffering a thousand deaths, thinking that I made some big mistake in the auction.

After a while I explained gently to them that a man has only one heart. I asked them to take pity on me and not to frown so much. We even arranged a code by which they could let me know how good the final contract was. Members of our team often switched from one language to another during a session and my idea was that if the contract was cold my partner should say *"Merci"* when I put down the dummy. If the contract was touch-and-go and might require some luck or good play, my partner would say *"Thank you."* Finally, if the contract was hopeless, the response to dummy's appearance would be *"Grazie."*

In a tournament in Deauville, I was partnering Pietro Forquet. After a very long auction, he arrived in a club grand slam. A trump was led and I put down the dummy.

*"Grazie,"* said Forquet.

"With a splendid dummy like that?" I cried. "How can it be *Grazie*?"

### BUSINESS BEFORE PLEASURE

When asked whether acting or bridge was more important to him, Omar Sharif replied "Acting is my business – bridge is my passion."

**Left:** Omar Sharif shows his hand during the Sunday Times International Bridge Pairs Championships, at the Hyde Park Hotel, London in 1980.

**Right:** A fine play by Omar Sharif at trick one. By ducking the first round of diamonds, Sharif ensures that his diamond entry cannot be removed.

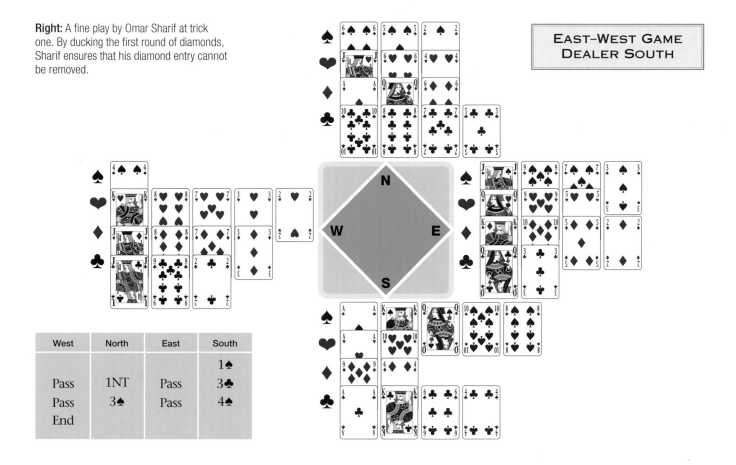

| West | North | East | South |
|------|-------|------|-------|
|  |  |  | 1♠ |
| Pass | 1NT | Pass | 3♣ |
| Pass | 3♠ | Pass | 4♠ |
| End |  |  |  |

Here is a deal that Omar played well, partnering Paul Chemla in a big tournament in the Deauville casino in France.

West led the ♦3 and Sharif made the excellent play of the ♦6 from dummy. East won but could not continue diamonds into dummy's tenace. He switched to a heart and Sharif won with the ace. When he played the ace and king of trumps, the position in that suit became clear. He crossed to the ♦A and took the marked finesse in trumps. When the clubs came in for only one loser, the game was his. Suppose West had turned up with four trumps to the jack and it was therefore necessary to dispose of the heart loser. Nothing would have been lost by the diamond play at Trick 1. Declarer could finesse the ♦Q on the second round of the suit!

You can see what would happen if declarer was tempted to play the ♦Q on the first trick. East would win with the ♦K and return the suit. When the two top trumps revealed the position in that suit, there would be no entry left to dummy to take a trump finesse.

Several years ago, Sharif underwent a heart triple bypass operation. He gave up playing top-level bridge and now lives a somewhat reclusive life in a Paris hotel. Still, suppose you step into a busy street in London or New York and ask the first passer-by who is the world's most famous bridge player. What answer are you likely to get? "Omar Sharif, isn't it?"

**Above:** Actor Omar Sharif at the start of the Macallan International Bridge Pairs Championship in 1997. Sharif joined a line-up of 32 top-class players competing for the trophy, a bottle of The Macallan whisky worth $19,500.

# HELEN SOBEL (USA)

There are several claimants for the title "greatest woman player ever" and the USA's Helen Sobel is certainly among them, having won 33 national championships. She won the McKenney Trophy, for most master points won in a calendar year, on three occasions. Between 1948 and 1964 she was the leading woman in the American Contract Bridge League's all-time master point rankings.

No one meeting a 16-year-old chorus girl in the Marx Brothers' show, *The Coconuts*, would have guessed that they were in the presence of a future great bridge champion. Chico Marx was, in fact, one of the best bridge players in show business. It was from a fellow chorus girl, however, that Sobel learnt the rudiments of bridge. After her first visit to a bridge club, she remarked to a friend, "You get to know something about trumps, playing pinochle, so I found bridge easy to pick up."

Sobel herself admitted that in her first couple of years of tournament play, she gained an advantage over any smug male opponents who might have taken her for a dumb blonde and expected soft pickings.

The word soon passed around that the "tiny blonde who looks like Gertrude Lawrence" played a very tough game indeed.

Her first marriage, at the age of 17, ended in divorce after just three years. It was a second marriage, to bridge expert Al Sobel, that was to change her life. Soon afterwards Ely Culbertson installed her as hostess at the Crockford's Club in New York, while her husband took over the editorship of the magazine *Bridge World*.

In 1937 Sobel was asked by Culbertson to join his team in a world championship event organized by the International Bridge League in Budapest. This was recognition indeed that both she and Josephine Culbertson were rated as the equal of any male player of the day.

Helen Sobel is probably most well known, however, for her enduring partnership with the great Charles Goren. Together they made an incredible team, and represented the USA in the 1957 Bermuda Bowl and the 1960 Olympiad.

Sobel's 33 national titles include the Spingold five times, the Chicago (now the Reisinger) four times and the Vanderbilt twice.

**Below:** Helen Sobel at the table. Edgar Kaplan, editor of *Bridge World*, said of her "In my lifetime, she is the only woman bridge player who was considered the best player in the world."

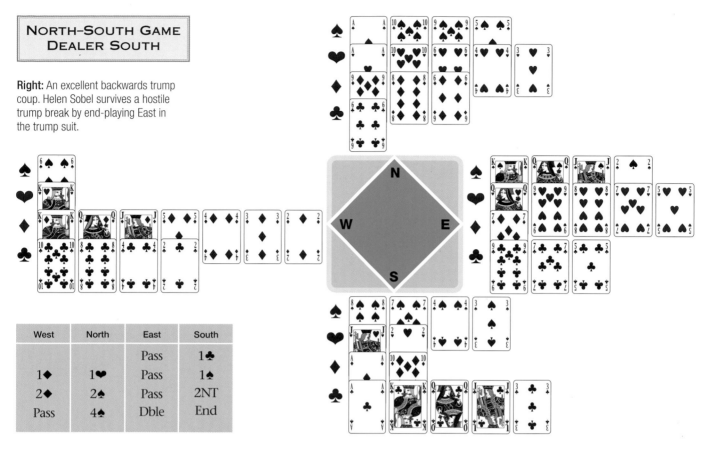

**NORTH–SOUTH GAME
DEALER SOUTH**

**Right:** An excellent backwards trump coup. Helen Sobel survives a hostile trump break by end-playing East in the trump suit.

| West | North | East | South |
|------|-------|------|-------|
| | | Pass | 1♣ |
| 1♦ | 1♥ | Pass | 1♠ |
| 2♦ | 2♠ | Pass | 2NT |
| Pass | 4♠ | Dble | End |

It's time for us to see an example of Sobel's dazzling card play, also her bravery in the bidding. The deal above shows her sitting South during the 1944 Summer Nationals.

Many players of the day would have refused to bid a spade suit of four cards to the eight. Helen Sobel not only bid the spades but continued to 2NT, over a single raise, on a hand that was not much more than a minimum. With a stack of trumps in his hand, East somewhat unwisely doubled the eventual spade game.

Sobel won the ♦K lead with the ♦A and played three rounds of clubs, discarding dummy's two diamond losers. She then led a heart, West's king appearing, and won with the ace in dummy. A second round of hearts was won by East's queen, West discarding a diamond. At this stage the defenders had one trick in the bag and it seemed likely that East would score three more with his ♠K–Q–J–2 poised over dummy's ♠A–10–9–5. See how the play developed, though.

East returned a heart and Sobel ruffed carefully with the ♠7, preventing an overruff from West's ♠6. She continued with a trump to the six, nine and jack. Declarer won the heart return in dummy, throwing the ♣3. She then led another heart, ruffing with the

♠4 in her hand. Trick 11 had been reached and East's last three cards were the ♠K–Q–2. Sobel ran the ♠8 to East's ♠Q and he was forced to lead a trump into dummy's ♠A–10 tenace at Trick 12. It was a splendid example of the technique known as a backward trump coup. If East's double had not alerted declarer to the bad trump break, it is unlikely that the winning line of play would have been found.

It was a source of minor aggravation to Sobel that the question most frequently asked of her, by worshippers of Charles Goren, was: "What is it like partnering a great player?" Her standard reply was: "Ask Charlie!"

---

**MAN'S WORLD**
♠ ♥ ♦ ♣

In an age where it was almost unheard of for women to compete at world level in open events, Helen Sobel was part of the USA open team that finished second in the World Team Championships in New York, 1957. She also finished fourth representing the USA open team at the 1960 World Team Olympiad, contested in Turin.

---

# INDEX